# BARCELONA
## CITY AND ARCHITECTURE
# 1980 - 1992

# BARCELONA
## CITY AND ARCHITECTURE
# 1980 - 1992

Oriol Bohigas

Peter Buchanan

Vittorio Magnago Lampugnani

RIZZOLI
NEW YORK

First published in the United States of America in 1991 by
Rizzoli International Publications, Inc.
300 Park Avenue South, New York, New York 10010

Library of Congress Cataloguing-in-Publication Data

Bohigas, Oriol.
Barcelona, city and architecture, 1980-1992 / Oriol Bohigas,
Peter Buchanan, Vittorio Magnano Lampugnani.

ISBN 0-8478-1354-1
    1. Architecture, Modern – 20th century – Spain – Barcelona.
2. Architecture – Spain – Barcelona. 3. Barcelona (Spain) –
Buildings, structures, etc. I. Buchanan, Peter. II. Magnano
Lampugnani, Vittorio, 1951. III. Title.
NA1311. B3B64 1991                                    90-24149
720'. 946' 4209048 – dc 20                            CIP


Translation: Graham Thomson

Cover design by Lanzagorta/Coma
Composition by Ormograf, S.A. – Barcelona
Color Separations by Reprocolor Llovet, S.A. – Barcelona
Printed in Spain by Grafos, S.A. – Barcelona

# Contents

# Publisher's foreword

The political and cultural changes of the last ten years and the nomination of Barcelona as host city for the 1992 Olympic Games have inspired an impressive number of architectural and urban design schemes. Along with the immediate need to construct specific buildings to house Olympic events, the city was determined to use the opportunity to move forward with projects for cultural buildings and facilities for city services, transportation, leisure and infrastructure. This considerable undertaking, still in progress, has involved the collaboration of a number of architects. Contributions by some of the most outstanding names in Barcelona's rich and varied professional scene and the involvement of invited architects of recognized standing from around the world have resulted, in our view, in a phenomenon of more than local interest.

All of these efforts are situated in the context of an existing city engaged in renewing its own fabric through an act of technical and political confidence in the potential of good design to improve the urban landscape.

The publishers of this collection, inevitably partial as it is, wish to express their thanks to all those individuals and institutions for the invaluable information and documentation they provided. At the same time, we regret the absence of documentation for the Auditorium designed by Spanish architect Rafael Moneo. This project rightly belonged in this selection, but the architect felt the scheme was not yet ready for publication.

# Notes on present-day urban design

## Vittorio Magnago Lampugnani

When Giuseppe Lanza, Duke of Camastra and Vicar-General of Val Demone and Val di Noto, founded a new city some seven kilometres from the ruins of the original Noto Antica, completely destroyed in the earthquake of 1693 barely a year before, he made use of an extremely simple procedure. Over the arid soil of the hill chosen for the *città di fondazione*, in the south-east of Sicily, he traced out the lines of the plan of a rational city, based on an orthogonal grid, at a scale of 1:1. The plots thus defined were shared out among the various property-owning citizens, with the conditions that they immediately construct at least the street facade of a building. In this way Noto Nuovo came into being, one of the most beautiful and enigmatic cities to be founded in the first part of the 18th century.

So much for legend; history, on the other hand, is much more complex and contradictory. The origins and principles of baroque utopian urban design, so spectacularly represented by Noto Nuovo, are to be found not so much in the philologically accurate as in the partially invented and simplified version of history. The first principle ought to be: a plan of the city which is geometrical and, if possible, compositionally elegant. The second principle: an architecture of uniform and, if possible, profusely decorated facades. The third principle is derived from the first two: a clearly defined urban space which can be taken in visually and traversed physically.

### The urban design of the present: cautious

If we cast an eye over the history and the present state of urban design, we cannot avoid the startling, to say the least, suspicion that these three principles, formulated in somewhat more general terms, are applicable to all cities in all times. The formula for a beautiful city seems to be unalterable: a good plan, an assortment of good buildings to fill it and, as a result, a suitable system of public spaces. To this we should add that the construction ought to be dense enough for the whole to be full of life. The only element that can be shifted around is the center of gravity: thus, for example, the Südliche Friedrichstadt district of Berlin, constructed by Philipp Gerlach in the 1730s, was based simply on a refined outline of the city, later converted into a space with the addition of comparatively insignificant facades. The Renaissance center of Rome, however, reveals a relatively insipid plan which owes its transformation into a grand sector of the city to the choice of architecture and nothing else.

So much for the historical city; but what about the modern city? Our way of life has changed profoundly in the course of the last hundred years, and above all over the last few decades. We now have millions of cars, which simultaneously encourage and impede the daily urban migration from home to workplace, along with new production and telecommunications technology, which have made this migration unnecessary and useless. Our habits as consumers have been considerably altered, and our rituals of leisure virtually revolutionized. Entirely new types of families live in houses which are given entirely new uses. In view of the new situation, can we still go on speaking of the same city as a hundred years ago, or will this too have to adapt and change profoundly?

Ever since the modern attack on the 19th century city, architects have not ceased to come up with utopian visions of the truly "new" metropolis as radical as they are fruitless, from the Ville Contemporaine to the Plug-in City. They have all failed because while people's way of life has changed, their basic needs and customs have not. The revolutions thought to be inevitable as a result of the mass consumption of new technical devices have not taken place: the television has not completely the theater or the cinema, and the telephone and telefax have certainly not rendered personal conversation obsolete, with all of the subtle shadings of meaning conveyed by face-to-face communication. Nor have the radical transformations of urban living predicted with such frequency taken us over completely. We travel by car, but we also walk and use public transport; we work at home, but in the office, too; we shop in the supermarket, but we still go to the little shop on the corner; we spend part of our free time within our four walls, but we go out, too. The newest forms of communal living are to be found in our homes alongside traditional family life. In our cities we see the coexistence side by side, and not infrequently in equal measure, of the most contrasting types – subversive and orthodox – of social life. Thus it is that people need traditional as well as new urban spaces, in which to carry on doing what they have been doing for hundreds and thousands of years: go for a stroll, see and be seen, meet and relate to other people. These activities are as ancient as the streets and public squares they need to take place in.

Another factor justifies the insistence on historic urban spaces. Europe has innumerable existing cities, and it is neither practicable nor necessary to demolish and rebuild them from the foundations up. What we are faced with, in any case, is the cautious renovation, modification and expansion of our cities. The architects and urban planners of the present are not now called upon to design a new city, as the Duke of

Camastra was three hundred years ago. What may seem as their more modest task is to find creative ways of conserving the existing city. It is not a question of conceiving but of caring for.

The urban design of the present emerges from a permanent conflict between the idea of a new city and the actual substance of an old city. This not only makes the undertaking more complex, but also more ambitious, since the idea has to be sufficiently strong to withstand the shock of collision with existing reality, yet at the same time modest enough to treat it with respect. A balance of this kind is not achieved through any formula, but must be found anew on every occasion and with each particular case. However, in light of the special set of problems facing contemporary urban design, basic principles which emerge from the parable of Noto can be expanded on and analyzed in greater detail.

## Great ideas

The remodelling of a city in terms of urban design and architecture must be directed towards what seems to be the highest imaginable ideal. In the final analysis, the goal is the planning and laying out of public spaces which have seen the evolution of human affairs over decades and centuries. Pragmatism which yields to supposed "objective imperatives" of the time has no justification.

A rejection of simple empiricism is far from being a piece of wishful thinking divorced from reality. Architecture takes as its object the realm of the possible: its dreams have to be achievable. The result of this circus balancing act is a concrete utopia which, far from any rigidity of mind or unreflecting luxury, proceeds to formulate architectonic and urban planning models for a happier and more just environment.

Within this framework, the history of architecture plays two quite different roles. On the one hand, it offers an immensely rich variety of established and unchanging solutions for the relationship between ways of living and architecture. On the other hand, precisely on account of this wealth of possibilities, it can easily lead to a complacent satisfaction with the existing state of affairs and a disinclination to look for anything beyond it. However, models for a happier and more just environment simply do not exist, and even if they did, only a process of permanent transformation could ensure their continuation as ideals throughout the course of history. The only

resolution of the dilemma between the resigned imitation of historical models and the delirious pursuit of "the new for its own sake" seems to be critical reflection of the greatest possible complexity and impartiality. It should consider the extent to which the reconstruction of the past points us towards the best possible future, and the extent to which the creation of new structures without precedent leads us towards a concrete utopia. Such reflection has to be undertaken both from the purely urban design point of view and from a far wider perspective.

Every new architectonic measure must be derived from the structural regularities already in existence in the city. The historic city's network of streets and squares will constitute the basis for any new interventions, which should elucidate and complement this existing grid. This reconstruction will seek to reestablish the urban form and layout of the past where it is valid and reasonable in terms of geometry, space and function. Where this is not viable, a new layout extrapolated from the existing one will be created with the aim of improving the historic city. The existing city should be understood to mean all that has been constructed in the city and has endured until the present. There is no such thing as a "good" or "bad" historical period; there are only good or bad measures with regard to a complex urban planning situation. The decision as to what should or should not be conserved and maintained will rest exclusively on urban design principles rather than philological ones. Isolated individual buildings must be subordinated to the regularity of the city. Only by taking its place within this framework can the individual building find full expression.

The new architectonic measures ought to render the history of the city as legible as possible, suggesting a "geological" stratification of the layers of its life as a community. A city is, amongst other things, a didactic construct, an instructive experience which speaks to us from its own memory. While there is no need for the new city to degenerate into some kind of pedantic exhibition of the past, it should give visible architectonic expression to the events experienced by the historic city, which destroyed and built it up, which shook and consolidated it, and so in all these ways formed it. Nothing which might go towards forming part of its future should be hidden away: a place is the sum of what it has been.

The objective of any architectural or urban design intervention is the creation, on the foundations of the past, of a new and rational city by means of a creative effort.

## Little ideas

As well as great ideas, today's urban development needs many little ones. For example, the principle of conservation, as opposed to that of new construction, requires sensitivity in approaching the existing fabric, whether adapting, modifying, expanding, completing or continuing. To do this it needs a concern for detail which does not come from theory but from craft alone. It is natural for a great idea, when truly great, to endure a certain degree of reduction or compromise, but the way in which it is put into effect is not a matter of indifference. In architecture and in urban design, material realization can never be considered in isolation from conception: one conditions the other. The same house can be quite different, depending on whether it is cast in plaster or clad in stone. The same city will be quite different, depending on whether its streets are paved in asphalt or cobbled.

In urban public space, detail plays a primordial part. Streetlights, benches, gardens, railings, fences, curbs and pavements often hold the citizen's attention more than monuments, facades or the configuration of public squares. Just like the policemen in Edgar Allan Poe's story *The Purloined Letter*, the citizen does not see the big things, only the small ones. Accordingly, the city's smallest details have to be planned, designed and produced with care.

## The city's face

Where is all this leading us? What is the higher objective to which these great and small ideas, these daring and cautious interventions in the historic city must all submit? Along what lines should the city be transformed? Every historic European city has its own face. This has evolved over the centuries as the result of innumerable political, social and architectural events, and reveals itself to a certain extent as the latest (and therefore never definitive) outcome of these events.

More than architects, the painters, film directors and poets are in the best position to recognize this face, as are outsiders rather than natives. This is never easy to define, far less simply on sight. Nevertheless, Franz Hessel, in *Spaziergänge durch Berlin*, produced an unmistakable portrait of the Prussian capital; Jean-Luc Godard has drawn an incredibly subtle profile of Paris in his various films; and Giorgio De Chirico outlined in paintings of his first period the quintessence of Turin.

An urban design which is not technocratic in character has to approach the city's face with care. What is involved is not some abstract utopia but a complex, subtle, and often hidden reality which must be recognized, developed, and, where there is good reason, modified. Altered, however, with care and sensitivity, because it consists not only of buildings, streets, squares, houses, monuments, parks, streetlights, billboards and paving stones, but also, and above all, of memories, experiences and dreams, or, in short, of life.

## Urban design with a sense of history: from Italy to Berlin

The first theoretical explorations of a solidly based contemporary urban design with a sense of history were carried out in Italy in the 1960s. These inquiries were to take the place of the modernist doctrine of the Athens Charter and its more or less technocratic derivatives. In the circles which included Saverio Muratore, Carlo Aymonino and, above all, Aldo Rossi, a new theory of urban design evolved which took as its starting point the historic European city, and from there went on to deduce the principles of a new approach to planning. The brothers Leon and Rob Krier took up these tenets, developed them in their own way and converted them into programmatic principles.

These researches were given their first tangible public expression at the International Architecture Exhibition in Berlin. From 1979 on, with the political pretext of an exhibition originally planned to take place in 1984 but postponed until 1987, it was decided to set about remodelling an extensive area of the former capital of Imperial Germany. A model program of urban refurbishment was planned in the historic sectors. In the new sectors, there was to be a no less exemplary process of urban renewal. Implicitly, the whole undertaking was directed at developing a prototype for the renovation of the European city.

Above all with regard to the new building sectors of Südliche Friedrichstadt and the Tiergartenviertel, to the south, the plan drawn up was relatively pragmatic, essentially oriented on an existing street layout where there was one, and on a historical model where there was not. Almost without exception existing buildings were left as they were, while construction schemes for the empty plots were invited from a variety of different architects, many with international reputations. These architects were asked to respect the alignment of the street or square and the particular building height established for the sector. Beyond these limitations, they were free to express their own artistic and architectural aims.

There can be no doubt that this magnificent experiment has, on balance, proved positive. From the political and cultural perspective, the International Architecture Exhibition acted as a point of encounter, confrontation and concord. In providing an opportunity for the concrete application and revision of new ideas, it played a decisive part in stimulating theoretical debate. From a design standpoint, it produced one of the most impressive collections of significant contemporary buildings in the world, some of them indisputable masterpieces.

A less enthusiastic response, however, must be accorded to the urban design work in the strict sense. The division into small scale sites, each constituting a separate brief, while intended to promote variety, proved in some areas to be an unfortunate move. Another factor was the architects' tendency to be as expressive as they could, so that in general the new districts look more like well laid out accumulations of isolated objects than parts of the city, and the main arteries create an impression which is often disturbing and at times disconcerting.

## The case of Barcelona

The *esprit de l'escalier* finds it easy to criticise. Nevertheless, the International Architecture Exhibition in Berlin, as a model of extremely rigorous and exigent urban design, was an immediately effective stimulus to other cities. Rome, Frankfurt-am-Main, Salzburg and even little Groninga in Holland projected, with varying degrees of success, ambitious architectural programs drawn up with the aim of refurbishing the city and the same time as a means of attracting attention to it. However, the city which took up the Berlin legacy in the most reflective, productive and intelligent manner was Barcelona.

With the death of General Francisco Franco and the creation of a favorable situation in the new democratic city councils, the Catalan capital was converted, almost overnight, into a gigantic architectural laboratory. This was largely due to the outstanding efforts on the architect Oriol Bohigas in his role as director of the city's Department of Architecture and Urban Design. The fundamental problem in Barcelona was different from that in Berlin, where the aim was to reconstruct entire sectors of the city which had been destroyed. Barcelona, on the whole well-conserved, needed an extremely focused refurbishment of individual points. Moreover, there was already a plan in existence for sector of the city known as the Eixample, drawn up

from 1859 onwards by the engineer Ildefons Cerdà, which was of much more practical value than the Hobrecht Plan for Berlin, and continued to dominate the urban form of the city.

With true Mediterranean pragmatism, Bohigas developed the urban design strategy of "benign metastasis": exemplary architectural schemes for individual points in need of refurbishment, which would help regenerate the surrounding urban environment by virtue of their positive influence. A considerable number of architects, most of them from Spain, committed themselves to designing projects, some remarkably small. In contrast to Berlin, where the construction of (subsidized) housing was the center of attention, in Barcelona public space was given top priority. Fewer houses were designed and built than main roads, and numerous public squares were redrawn, transformed and embellished. Slowly but surely large scale urban projects were undertaken (the Moll de la Fusta, by Manuel de Solà-Morales; the Bac de Roda-Felip II bridge by Santiago Calatrava, and others). The *res publica* was urbanistically and architecturally fêted with a refined minimalism.

The urban design and planning operation for the 1992 Olympic Games is on a different scale. Just as in Berlin, a one-off event was taken as the pretext for setting in motion a fundamental and lasting transformation of the city, and just as in Berlin, the strategy had its own traditions. While the International Architecture Exhibition could look back to the Städtebau-Ausstellung of 1910, the Deutsche Bauausstellung of 1930 and the Interbau of 1957, Barcelona's Vila Olímpica looks back to its Universal Exposition of 1888 and the International Exhibition of 1929.

The planning and construction of the sports installations (the Olympic Ring) on the hill of Montjuïc were entrusted to a group of architects from Spain and abroad, including Federico Correa, Vittorio Gregotti and Arata Isozaki. Additional installations are projected for the western extreme of the Diagonal, Barcelona's main thoroughfare, and for the Vall d'Hebron area. However, the heart of the new urban planning work taking place here is the site of almost 124 acres between the Ciutadella Park and the Poble Nou district, to the north-east of the city, which will be transformed into the new neighorhood of Nova Icària, in line with the plan by Josep Martorell, Oriol Bohigas, David Mackay and Albert Puigdomènech.

The structure of the city as drawn by Cerdà, with its residential blocks 371 × 371 feet in area, will be conserved in principle. It will be somewhat contaminated, however, with elements of the functionalist

Macià Plan, elaborated by the rationalist grove of Catalan architects known as GATCPAC, in conjunction with Le Corbusier. The main contributions taken from the Macià Plan are the "superblock" complexes with their great landscaped interior spaces, pedestrian walkways set at a distance from traffic routes, and rows of detached houses and isolated pavilions. Is this Ville Verte adapted to Barcelona conditions, the change of scale of the urban structure implied a modification of the street form and the role of architecture, which was not to be used to define the public space. In the Nova Icària however, this same change of scale has the objective of conserving the traditional urban configuration and making it compatible with the new functional typologies. The clean smooth break is replaced by complex mediation.

To what extent Nova Icària proves to be a success will be evident in 1992, when the greater part of the work is completed. On the one hand, the reconciliatory synthesis of two contrasting models of historic city and the modern city seems to harbor a danger that justice will not be done to either, or that both will be obliged to accept too many compromises. On the other hand, the experiment of combining the principles of the traditional city, with its clearly delimited and easily recognized public spaces, and those of the functionalist city, with its light, peaceful housing and semi-public areas designed for families, is the challenge faced by planners at the end of this century. Nova Icària, no matter how successful or otherwise its actual realization turns out to be, will make a decisive contribution to the progress of this experiment.

**Perspectives: the city of tolerance**

At present, Berlin and Barcelona are the two most important test laboratories for contemporary architecture and urban design: one with a markedly international and pluralist orientation, the other with a more regionalist, though decidedly undogmatic, character. Going beyond what is specific to the cultural strategy adopted in each case, and the distinctive "face" of either city, what seems to be taking place in both is nothing other than that process foreseen by Robert Musil back in the thirties, without reference to any particular city (since "no special importance" was to be attached to the name):

> As in all great cities, this one contained irregularities, changes, advances, maladjustment, collisions of things and affairs, immense areas of silence,

impassable roads and places, a great rhythmic pulse and the eternal dissonance and dislocation of every rhythm, and was on the whole like a bubble expanding in a receptacle composed of the solid substance of houses, laws, decrees and historical traditions.

We are dealing here, of course, with the traditional city (which is still the only place where a truly urban way of life is possible) as a city of contradictions; yet also as the city of tolerance. Perhaps the juxtaposition of a variety of different architectures in Berlin and Barcelona symbolizes precisely that: the coexistence of different conceptions and ways of life. If this is so, they are outlining nothing less than the profile which the city of the present should adopt with regard to the future.

# Architecture for sport in Catalonia

## Oriol Bohigas

Sport, in its dual character as activity and spectacle, has a relatively long and important tradition in Catalonia, above all when compared with the rest of Spain. There is little point in seeking out historical or picturesque examples such as that of the Barcelonese Lucius Minicius Natalis, who in 129 A.D. won a quadriga race in the 227th Olympics, since such examples belong to a context in which Catalonia did not yet exist as a sociocultural reality. However, without going beyond the limits of what we might call modernity, it is quite evident that Catalonia has long been in the vanguard of an approach to sport which is at once popular and intellectualized on the one hand, there was the founding of the Barcelona Football Club, and on the other, the lengthy tradition – controversial, and at times charged with political ideas – of open air schools and school camps at the beginning of this century, along with the ethical and aesthetic tone of the ramblers' societies, whose excursions focussed on sport and archaeology. This dual character of Catalan sport is marked by a cosmopolitan attitude, with its origins in the institutionalization of Catalanism, developed out of the twin bases of bourgeois industrialism and the ideology of *Noucentisme.* At the same time as Joan Miró was taking lessons in boxing from Hemingway, Pere Verges, following Manuel Ainaud's initiative, was running a school on the Barceloneta beach where ecological rhythms – and their derivations in sport – were extolled as pedagogical principles. While Joan Gamper's club – founder of Barcelona Football Club – triggered an early explosion of popular interest in sport, and the first tennis, golf and swimming clubs were appearing on the scene, the complicated genesis of the 1929 International Exposition was accompanied by persistent calls for the Olympics to be brought to Barcelona. This was against the backdrop of ascendant Nazism in Germany, along with French and English indecisiveness, precursors to the hypocritical "non-intervention" policy and its inevitable and tragic consequences in the Spanish Civil War.

Even after the organization of sport was brought under the control of state structures, Catalonia maintained – and still maintains – a relative operational autonomy. A considerable number of federations originated and developed inside Catalonia, which were often, during Franco's dictatorship, the last reserves – and the only symptom – of a social and cultural decentralization at variance with the objectives reality of the regime. It is hardly surprising, then, that Catalonia – that is to say, Barcelona – should have had relevant and significant experience, and a degree of primacy, in the design and construction of spaces and buildings for sport. This was in spite of the huge cultural parenthesis which was Francoism, and the scarcity of economic and human resources at the disposal of Catalan institutions.

It would be no easy task to draw up a genealogy of modern sports construction in Barcelona, but there are two major buildings which are capable between them of explaining the genre: Barcelona Football Club's Camp Nou stadium, together with its various annexes, and the Montjuïc stadium built for the 1929 International Exposition. Barça's present facilities are the latest in a long series: the Sants ground, the one in Les Corts (subsequently transformed with the addition of a magnificent stand build by the engineer Eduardo Torroja, and a contribution by the architect Eusebi Bona which was more bureaucratic than real) and the Nou Camp (the work of Francesc Mitjans, again with some fairly bureaucratic assistance, in this case from Josep Soteras and Lorenzo García-Barbón), along with the mini-stadium and the Blaugrana sports hall, which today make up the most important complex of sports facilities in Spain. This complex was wholly funded by an extremely numerous and enthusiastic group of citizens, a private entity which has, as is often the case in the cultural life of Barcelona, won official patronage with the slogan, *"el Barça és més que un club"* – Barça is more than a club.

The old stadium on Montjuïc is doubly significant: as an architectonic object, and at the same time as expression of civic intention. It is – or was, prior to its last transformation – an interesting building in that it simultaneously explored a number of lines which were contradictory even by the eclectic standards of its time. On the one hand, its setting in the landscape was rather unusual: almost on the summit of a hill, with a very open layout, such that the interior of its concave space seemed to be an interpretation, in landscape terms, of the classical amphitheaters. This was despite the fact that the pretentious, and even somewhat careless, adaptation to the site was carried out by the use of a contrived device, the laying-out of sports tracks and a grass pitch on top of a roof resting on metal columns. On the other hand, however, this simple modulation of the landscape was disguised on the exterior with a facade whose intentions are quite manifestly urban. What is not known is whether this was the result of a deliberate attempt at monumentalizing the Montjuïc hill in an "urban" manner (a fairly evident aim of later projects for the Exposition, from the phase designed by Puig i Cadafalch and Cambó to that by Domènech i Roura and Barón de Viver) or simply because the stylistic approach of the architects employed on the second phase was akin to a Beaux Arts mode steeped in nostalgia for Central European baroque, with a vocabulary appropriate only to post-Hausmannian squares and avenues.

Beyond these questions of form and style there is, as remarked above, another significant ingredient. The construction of the old stadium was directly related to the petition to hold the Olympic Games in Barcelona, the concession of which was delayed time and again, until Hitler's Berlin commandeered the 1936 Games. This occurred while Spain was tearing itself apart in the Civil War, able only to mount – and then immediately interrupt – the Popular Olympiad on Montjuïc as a modest international counterpoint to the Nazi festival. However, in spite of the frustration of its primary objectives, the stadium assumed a representative role and characteristic profile in the city. It was a much loved meeting place for the unassuming athletes of the forties, fifties and sixties, upholders of the old educational and civic spirit, until neglect and misuse finally put an end to it.

For all of these reasons, it was decided, quite rightly, to construct the new stadium for the 1992 Olympic Games as a remodelling of the old fabric, conserving as far as possible the image and the profile which has for so long been a part of the city's history and symbolism. This was the basic premise of the limited international competition for the design of all the sports buildings, and the laying out of the so-called Olympic Ring on Montjuïc.

The two proposals which best coordinated the conservation of the old image with a radical approach to the new facility were the scheme by Vittorio Gregotti and the one by Correa-Milá-Buxadé-Margarit. The jury suggested that these two teams work together on a definitive project. The results of their collaboration – which must undoubtedly have had its internal difficulties – have been interesting and, above all, extremely pertinent. The skin of the facade has been retained almost in its entirety, while at the same time the interior, demolished and then rebuilt from scratch, reinterprets – with a better image and improved construction – the spatial expansion and subtle reference to classical colonies, following the morphology found in the settlements on the exposed hilltops of the Mediterranean. Moreover, both outer shell and content put forward a risky but interesting, and above all fruitful dialectic, which is at its most pronounced in two essential elements: the great girder above and at the back of the main facade, and the two alignments of the banked seating, so explicitly differentiated. The girder, of a brilliant, antiseptic whiteness, establishes a new role for the facade, which now cannot be reduced like a cardboard cut-out to a mere plane surface, as it decorously acknowledges and assimilates the issue of the interferences. The alignment of tiers of seating in the upper stand follows the broken curves of the old facade, while the seating in the lower stand maintains the continuity of line of the track surround. The intermediary spaces produced between these two alignments run the full depth of the building, provide extremely good support and with vertical sequences and the entry of light determine the space typical of

an open air sports ground, open to the continuity of the landscape and the sky, to rain and sun, and to unrestricted communication between the general public outside and the spectators inside. This, undoubtedly, is the finest quality of the Montjuïc Olympic Stadium: that of being an open space, with neither physical nor psychological barriers, like a stretch of hillside, slightly hollowed out to enable athletes and spectators to compete according to ethical principles and the bases of a democratic dialogue, germane to what a communal sporting event really ought to be. It is to be regretted, however, that the latest modifications imposed by strict security precautions required by athletes and politicians are now reducing the transparency and fluidity of the space, so that some of the initial concepts are now less explicit.

The competition for the design of the Olympic Ring referred above produced another very positive result: the awarding of the commission for the Sant Jordi sports pavilion to the Japanese architect Arata Isozaki. As mentioned, the competiton was held with the intention of commissioning a single winner for the entire plan and complex of buildings, but the jury had sufficient good sense to award each project to a different architect within the overall urban plan proposed by the team of Correa-Milá-Buxadé-Margarit. This was the right decision for two reasons: because in this way the complex took on a form composed of relatively autonomous architectures – as befits the traditional morphology of Montjuïc – and because it obliged each architect to reconsider his project from an urban design angle and, in so doing, get rid of the preconceptions which tend to be generated by competitions, often unduly absorbing and remote from the dialectics of production and use.

Arata Isozaki's Palau is without doubt a masterpiece, surely because the new landscaping scheme, and dialectical relationships with the various realities of the setting, demanded a very positive degree of response. In the first design sketch the great shell of the roof had a suggestive reference to various branches of European expressionism (and certain Japanese formal reminiscences). It all seems much more pertinent now, not only with reference to the formal order of the great square which is the backbone of the Olympic Ring, but to the functional structure itself and the various ways the building can be used. Certain problems of scale have been improved, too. Thus the expressive sinuosities are apparent from close up, while the massive volume displays subtlety of a different dimension, in which the axes of its situation and its corporeal substance set up a coherent dialogue with the hill itself and even with the city skyline.

One could, indeed, analyze the expressive use of technology present here within a tendency which shuns both the intestinal radicalism of high-tech and the bulges of its clean, decorated outer casing. I know, of course, that this attitude is very frequent in Arata Isozaki's work, but it seems to me that on Montjuïc he adopts a more direct language, with fewer superficial resources and less rhetoric. I have no hesitation in affirming that this sports pavilion constitutes a significant milestone in Isozaki's work. It radically distances itself from certain temptations discernible in the ornamental quality of historicist and populist allusion, references which at times, in oriental culture, expose themselves to ridicule through an excessively literal use of western elements, attributable either to modesty or hauteur. Compared with the Italianizing quotations of the Tsukuba City Hall, or the ornamental deliquescence of the Sala Pau Casals, the austerity of the Palau Sant Jordi displays considerable ethical and architectonic progress.

The stadium and Palau relate to each other by way of a great public space designed by the Correa-Milá-Buxadé-Margarit team, consisting of a square, garden, line of monuments, and functional plinth. This is magnificent ordering matrix in which they have achieved the elusive combination of an immediately legible monumentality and a tense dislocation of axes and routes. A complex formal composition results, calling for a more sophisticated reading. In addition to the rare quality of the space, what should be emphasized is the simple fact that the space exists and has been designed with such an imposing character.

One of the successes of Barcelona's latest, or perhaps, now, second-latest policy in urban design has been the attempt to design the city starting from public space. This attempt would have no meaning were it not accompanied by other criteria which posit the role of public space in terms of higher structures, such as the dialogue between center and periphery, the relationship to amenities, the sectorial vision of the asystemic nature of the city, and the new unifying and legitimating value of the plan. Nevertheless, public space has been the fundamental issue in designing the city, or, at least, its most effective aspect. The Olympic Ring on Montjuïc also acknowledges the priority of public space, and, for all the individuality of each building, may well be the first Olympic complex organized around this criterion.

Even in buildings situated at some distance from the formal urban structure, concern with surroundings has been of overriding importance. One characteristic example is the Velòdrom cycle track in Vall d'Hebron, the work of Bonell and Rius, the first sports facility built here with a view to the Olympic Games. The problem here is the siting of a geometric form with difficult connections to hazardous terrain – since the public works nearby have caused it to lose its original

structure – without any legible geographical composition from an architectural point of view. The incorporation of the essential form within a cylinder with a circular base, emerging radically from the sloping surface of the terrain, and the clearly monumental treatment of the surroundings – sculpture starting out from a visual poem by Brossa, a flight of steps and an entrance archway to the neighboring Laberint maza and gardens – resolve the problem precisely on the basis of their global conception of the exterior space.

The new facilities now under construction in this same Vall d'Hebron sector are also the result of a prior arrangement of public space. The projects for the sports complex by Garcés and Sòria, tennis courts by Tonet Sunyer and archery grounds by Enric Miralles are all installations which derive from an ordering of the terrain (in this instance drawn up by Eduard Bru with a very precise design) despite having moved away from a more traditional urban language, as in the formally defined city and formally definable new districts which dovetail with the city and seek to extend it without resolution. This sector of the Vall d'Hebron will draw – by contrast with what is taking place in the Vila Olímpica, for example – on another tradition: that of the well-planned suburb, in which the fragmentation of the architectonic episodes elucidates a different continuity, encouraging a new expression of landscape in the transition from city to ordered geography.

The Velòdrom can also be explained, in more stylistic terms, as an approximation to naked forms, only here and there vibrated or altered as minimal forms – which does not mean "minimal" in the art-history sense – according to a deliberately limited repertoire widely used by a considerable number of architects of the sixties generation (or might we call it, following Ortega, the generation of '65, given that its predecessor was the fifties generation?), many of whom have designed sports buildings of one kind or another. In any case, we would need to establish, within this generational grouping, certain differences in the relatively generalized use of minimalist and reductionist language.

The sixties generation has an evident, immediate potency in Catalonia, and offers – within a certain inescapable geographical and temporal unity, although this sometimes seems hard to see at such close quarters – an interesting diversity of tendencies which are precisely those responsible for the dissolution of the so-called Barcelona School, still based on the stylistic and almost strictly codified expression of realism. Oscar Tusquets and Ricardo Bofill, for example, belong to this generation, although they have made their separate getaways along the path of classsical and romantic literature, while the

17

inclusion of Lluís Clotet and Esteve Bonell, surely two of the most mature figures on the Spanish scene, have a significance more amenable to generalization. They, like Rafael Moneo and Juan Navarro Baldeweg in the Madrid group, and Luis Peña in San Sebastián, have found means of expression more suited to the vicissitudes of construction, and function within a program still optimistic and purposeful – modern, when all is said and done – with regard to the progress of forms and contents. Whithin this same generation, meanwhile, Helio Piñón and Albert Viaplana mount their attack – intelligent, skilled, the initiators of new sensibilities for new formal catalogues – through atomizing decomposition and volleys charged with signification, at same time as they aim, and in their case it is true, at a certain minimalism. Finally there are those who, like Jordi Garcés and Enric Sòria, adopt a systematic mutism, in a attempt at avoiding problems and contradictions rather than underlining and resolving them, almost assuming the asepsis of a "less is less" approach.

Between these four poles there are quarter points to which other allusions are often added – minimal ornamentalism as a homoepathic homage to *Modernism*, the Secession and Art Deco; the hardness of a contained high-tech; a nostalgia for the utopia of the Bauhaus; the less than ingenuous regionalisms; the syncretisms intended to smooth away faltering hesitation – to make up a complex and highly interesting panorama. There are architects such as Bach-Mora, Espinet-Ubach, Bosch-Tarrús-Vives, Dani Freixes, Manuel Brullet, Eduard Bru, Josep L. Mateo, Antoni de Moragas, Javier San José, Pepe Llinás and so many others who together constitute a complicated interweaving of lines. Within this framework, attention must be given to the subtle nuances of younger figures such as Tonet Sunyer, Enric Miralles, Galí-Quintana, Fernández-Gallego, Yago Conde and so on: in other words, what we might call the eighties generation.

Out of all this multiplicity – less disperse than it might appear – the most interesting position is that posited on the work of Clotet and Bonell. They open up simultaneously new perspectives of "seny" and "rauxa", of good sense and impulsiveness, of traditional progressiveness and the traditional critique of the traditional, to this writer, Clotet and Bonell – along with their noteworthy accomplices – are the best Catalan architects of their generation, and one of them, Clotet, seems to be the most clearsighted of recent years with regard to the posing of ethical and cultural problems in European architecture. Clotet is surely, together with Rafael Moneo, the most acute critical observer of present-day architecture, at least within the field of Spanish culture. He has written only a very few texts, but all of them situated on that point of intersection which defines recent history and its perspectives. Texts,

above all, which elucidate not only the evolution of his architecture in its entirety but the abiding presence of ethical and political convictions. Clotet must be the only architect of his generation who has managed to evolve within his architecture, without throwing his ethical principles overboard in favor of an idea of progress based on rationalism, optimism and faith in the transformative potential of society, or of certain segments of society.

The Velòdrom in the Vall d'Hebron is an obvious, even programmatic, result of this professional and intellectual position. So, too, is Bonell and Rius' Municipal Sports Center in Badalona. Here, the problems are resolved rather than eliminated. The structure is not a necessary and superable encumbrance, as it is in Ricardo Bofill's new Barcelona Airport, or in some of the work by the young adherents of bulging, machine-like form, but a substantial constituent of the expressive process. The relationship with the environment is neither the haughty disdain of Calatrava's Telefónica tower in the Olympic Ring, nor the formal mimesis of the dyed-in-the-wool conservatives, but a proposal for a new reading, a reading which is at once legible and corroborative. Within the same compositional scheme we find indications which endorse this commitment. There is the curving of the outer skin, with its technical references to craft tradition, going on to metamorphose into a structural rectangle, where the change of form is at the same time a change of language, an act of juggling involving both craftsmanship and a version of high-tech which is neither overly aggressive nor pretentious. The Badalona Sports Center will certainly become an architectural landmark – and a programmatic proposal – as important as the Velòdrom in the Vall d'Hebron, or the Stadium and Palau Sant Jordi, on Montjuïc have proved to be.

Many of the sports complexes built in Catalonia in recent years have been designed by architects of the sixties generation, which has had the good fortune to receive a considerable number of commissions from official bodies. All of these architects, in addition to resolving the specific architectural question in terms of the line aimed at defining here, have also focussed on the more urban dimensions of that question. Bach and Mora's work in Perill street in the district of Gràcia, for example, paves the way for the rehabilitation and reconstruction of a whole neighborhood, making intelligent use of residual spaces in blocks which are either incomplete or unevenly utilized. Espinet and Ubach's Renfe-Meridiana sports complex is resolved as an element which links together, as far as possible, residential areas fragmented by the existing anti-urban planning and a lack of facilities and identifying marks.

On an even greater urban scale and, accordingly, with a clearly metropolitan significance, we ought next to consider the leisure port being built alongside the Olympic Village. The construction of an entire neighborhood from scratch is a risky undertaking, because of the difficulty of ensuring what we might call the "naturalness" of its future forms of occupation and use. A new neighborhood ought to be like any other neighborhood born out of the superimpositions, changes, flexibilities and even contradictions brought by the slow, accumulative process of history over the years. A living thing has to be created, but "in vitro". The project for the Olympic Village tries to confront this problem through the use of a variety of means, not only of design but of management: the continuity of urban texture, the mixture of uses, the multiplicity of a group of coordinated designers, the reconsideration of legible morphologies in spite of the presence of new residential typologies, the clarity and amplitude of its communications with the center and with the rest of the metropolitan complex, and so on.

Nevertheless, in order to consolidate this new centrality, it was of fundamental importance to locate a number of "motors" of concentrated, permanent activity. In this respect, the inclusion of a major shopping center, hotels with their conference facilities and, above all, the leisure port, with its moorings and dry dock, schools for water sports, shops, restaurants, facilities and services for high-level competitions was a basic objective of the project. In the first design sketch, only a small area for temporary moorings was envisaged, a space with neither the structure nor the form of a port because it was conceived as a kind of marine piazza for public use, like a maritime continuation of the parks and squares along the seafront. However, as the project moved on to deal with programs for use, and looked more deeply at the envisaged functions and social content for the aftermath of the Olympic Games, it became apparent that this "marine piazza" would have to take on the role of promoting these permanent activities for the whole of the new neighborhood. Thus the conception changed to that of a leisure port, in which, however, the urban functions derived from the entire coastal structure would prevail. In other words, a port with highly demanding functional requirements but, at the same time, a thoroughly architectural image and configuration, with the same methods and the same objectives as those employed in the development of the policy for public spaces in all the neighborhoods of Barcelona.

It would not be too much of an exaggeration to say that this port is one of the few to be designed and constructed on the basis of the very balanced involvement of a number of specialists: architects Martorell-Bohigas-Mackay-Puigdomènech and civil engineer J. Ramón de Clascá, orchestrating a fairly complex team of specialists of different kinds, working together towards the realization of the twin objectives proposed. With this scheme, Barcelona surely has achieved the maximization of its urban design policy, in that the criteria of an approach to town planning, marked by a priority given to the design of public space, has reached extraordinary dimensions. As a rule, modern ports come into being as sterile containers for mercantile, industrial or recreational functions, to be used subsequently as urban bases once these functions have drifted into total or partial obsolence, that is, when their function as port has drifted towards a function as urban space. This has been the origin of new uses for ports in Europe and America, where very often the frenzy of unrestrained speculation has disfigured the normal possibilities for transforming the uses of the old harbor facilities. In Barcelona itself at this moment there is an important debate about the development of – and prior or subsequent speculation in – the old port, in which the problems of appropriateness are fundamental. The aim of the Olympic Port is to try to attain in the first instance the ultimate objective, which is to say, to directly construct an urban setting within a maritime environment. Of course there are many seafront leisure facilities which have achieved this goal, but here we have in addition both the metropolitan dimension and the role of the port as "motor" to the performance of an entire neighborhood, whose future will be determined by the urban effectiveness of these activities.

# Monuments to a classic-constructivist civitas

**Peter Buchanan**

1983 saw the completion of the Plaça Sants in front of Barcelona's main railway station –the event that first riveted to the city the attention of architects everywhere. Yet the inspired brilliance of the plaza's design is only part of the reason that it hailed the notice the city has enjoyed ever since. Much of this might best be explained by the fact that the same year saw too the fiftieth anniversary of the Charter of Athens. The resulting reassessments had brought to a head an increasing awareness of just how devastating its well intended and once seemingly rational proposals had proved. European cities, and those elsewhere, had been torn apart to segregate "the four functions of work, home, recreation and movement". Architecture had been reduced to buildings free-standing in a void, quite devoid of any connections (physical, formal or rhetorical) with history or context. To this catastrophic destruction of the crucibles and legacy of European culture, Barcelona now offers an inspiring alternative.

Though a good deal of the mess of the city's newer periphery and extensions is attributable to Charter of Athens type thinking, Barcelona's central areas have largely been spared the ravages of such planning. Decades of public sector neglect and unchecked private sector speculation during the Franco era however had left the city run down, very densely built and inhabited, and desperately deprived of public facilities. Since the coming of democracy, Barcelona has been upgrading itself to rectify past deficiencies and serve its now more affluent and aspiring citizens. An ambitious program is under way, building such new social facilities as schools, sports halls, parks and plazas. Hosting the Olympic Games is part of and has given further impetus to this process, which also includes the refurbishment and expansion of major cultural monuments. This is the context in which all recent architecture included in this book must be understood. It is part of a public sector strategy that has generated a private sector response in building new hotels and housing, which has filtered down to a general sprucing up of the whole city.

Instead of constructing the type of new roads and buildings that cause a city to splinter into mono-functional fragments, Barcelona is reintegrating and enriching both its urban fabric and the civic experience of its inhabitants. The old city is being opened up, but not by obstructive voids for only cars to rush through. Networks of public places are being threaded through the old and new city for people to promenade, pause and play in. These are not isolating single-use barriers but multi-functional foci of pedestrian connection as well as of social and visual cohesion. These networks are sited where opportunities allow, and wherever possible along or close to the social and cultural facilities are being provided in new, refurbished or expanded buildings.

While the public realm of so many cities is deteriorating, or even being deliberately destroyed and/or privatized, Barcelona stands out for expanding and enriching its public realm with proper concern for the city's spatial and symbolic quality. Some though may see the emphasis on public life, especially in plazas where it is both out of doors and outside of any market function, as anachronistic. Yet, if also fuelled by a certain Catalan chauvinism, there is nothing nostalgic about the strategy being pursued or its products, even when these evoke or actually re-use components (such as nineteenth-century lamp posts) from the past or conserve old buildings. Much of the excitement about what is happening in Barcelona is precisely because it is redefining a particularly vivid vision of civic life in the late twentieth century. More than that, this vision is both throughly modern, yet essentially Mediterranean; celebrating hedonistic civic traditions that were themselves an original inspiration to certain phases of Modernism.

Barcelona's new public architecture and open spaces, a selection of which constitutes the subject of this book, thrill then for their poise between past and future, often fusing familiar archetypal and avant-garde forms. At one level, there is a pleasing frisson in the conjunction of astringently minimalist form, and the solid satisfactions of traditional materials, crafted construction and detail. At another level, even the most abstracted and fragmented forms tend to have, no matter how muted or transmuted, some recognizable roots in and resonances with the past. This crucial quality allows these new works (unlike the architecture and urbanism associated with the Charter of Athens) to complement and make coherent connections to, even while contrasting with, local context and culture. A lack of this quality in projects by foreign architects, who simply do their usual thing, engaging locality at only the most superficial of formal levels, leaves their works so much less interesting than the best of those by local architects. A combination of all the positive qualities described above elevates recent Barcelona architecture far above the impoverished caricatures of Neo-Rationalism, Neo-Vernacular and Post-Modernism. These were the responses elsewhere to the degradation wrought by Modernism and the Charter of Athens. All of them of course had some influence in Barcelona, but usually too well digested to be readily discernible.

Barcelona's urban renaissance is part of a general flowering of creative talent unleashed by the end of the restrictive Franco era. But its roots run deeper than this or the influence of contemporary theory and example from elsewhere. Spain has its own legacy of outstanding modern architects that inspire those working today. Especially important for Barcelona is José Antonio Coderch (1913-1984), who today would be called a Regionalist. He used traditional motifs and planning devices to create an architecture suited to and evoking some spirit of the Mediterranean. He also invented types and devices of his own that have been taken up by other architects for their aptness to and resonances with local conditions.

Since its beginnings in Barcelona modern architecture has been tempered to local tradition and conditions to create a vital hybrid. GATCPAC's Casa Bloc folds the free-standing slab to respect both the street wall and create courtyards off it, while Sert, Torres & Subirana's Tuberculosis clinic is entered through a patio with a cool tiled and shaded ambulatory. Later, in the fifties and inspired by Italian Neo-Realism, Antoni Moragas of Group R advocated a hybrid of traditional forms and materials used in an abstract modern manner. Two young members of Group R were Oriol Bohigas and Josep Martorell who are now principals, with David Mackay, of Martorell/Bohigas/Mackay (MBM).

Both as a practice and in the activities of its individual partners, especially Oriol Bohigas, MBM has played a crucial role in shaping contemporary Barcelona architecture. All three partners have written historical studies and other books on architecture, while the practice's work remains true to its Group R origins in using traditional materials and devices to create a Regionalist Modernism. The interest in history and tradition, openness to foreign ideas and discriminating eclecticism all typify Barcelona architecture today. This has benefited immensely from its incubation in the creative climate MBM helped create towards the end of and after the Franco era.

Bohigas played more direct roles too. He was for some time director of la Escola Tècnica Superior d'Arquitectura de Barcelona where most of the architects featured in this book studied. Those who trained before this period benefited from teaching there with Bohigas and Rafael Moneo. A critical influence on many of his teaching colleagues Moneo, like Bohigas, stresses the importance of history and local precedent. So a prime influence on its architects is Barcelona itself,

with its fascinating urban morphology and wildly vigorous and eclectic architectural heritage. Not least of this is the *Modernisme* period that, besides Gaudí, includes Puig i Cadafalch, Domènech i Montaner and Jujol. The work of Jujol in particular has been an enthusiasm of several of the architects included here. Though there is little direct influence, it is taken by young architects such as Enric Miralles & Carme Pinós to legitimate their own experimental approaches. And prior to the *Modernisme* period, Catalan architecture was characterised by a spareness of form and austerity of finish – qualities found in much recent work in Barcelona.

Later Bohigas became the city's director of urban projects and initiated the process whereby Barcelona began to regenerate its urban fabric. Instead of formulating and following some rigid grand plan, he seized local opportunities to initiate a staggering series of projects, guided only by a flexible overall strategy. Yet his contribution was not just in an opportunistic pragmatism allied with imagination and charisma, but also in the sensitivity with which he matched commissions to architects – most of whose talents he was well aware of as ex-students or fellow teachers. This process has been continued by his successor Josep Acebillo and extended into such provincial departments as those commissioning health centers and schools.

The conscientious commissioning of talented architects that came with democracy and the air of adventure that surrounded the whole enterprise was part of a general flirtation and alliance among fellow intellectuals, joining socialist politicians with avant-garde artists and architects, an effort largely catalyzed by Bohigas as well as by chauvinist pride. Together they would rebuild not just the social and physical fabric, but cultural and artistic life too. The enthusiastic endorsement of the artistic is what licenses the vigorous diversity of expression of the new architectures which must not just serve but also symbolize new aspirations. The new public facilities are then also monuments to both the new civic vision and the cultured emancipated citizen, to whom there is no need to pander with an easy and overly explicit populism.

The resultant diversity of expression now found in Barcelona should not be confused with the usual pluralist gamut of fashionable styles found elsewhere. For beneath the variety are the communalities already described, the most important of which are those of civic vision and the evoked connections with context and culture. Besides, despite the diversity, much of the best architecture, in seeking to serve these qualities also tends towards one or the other of two contrasting compositional approaches. These might be characterized as the classical and the constructivist. The former exploits or slyly subverts the symmetrical, repetitive order and the decorative motifs of this very familiar and archetypally Mediterranean style. Leading exponents of this approach are Esteve Bonell & Francesc Rius and Jaume Bach & Gabriel Mora, Bofill's Taller d'Arquitectura practices a more bombastically overblown classicism, that lacks the refinement and elegance of the work of these two partnerships. Much of Madrid architect Rafael Moneo's work gets its resonance from classical allusions and/or discipline, and also reminds us that a now dimly distant inspiration for this approach was the theory and example of Aldo Rossi.

If the classical tends to self-containment and is an essentially architectural approach, the constructivist pole is essentially sculptural and is more directly connected, if only by gestural inflection, to the surroundings from which it is generated. It is then a contextual approach, but not in the conventional sense of achieving continuities with neighboring buildings. Instead it delineates and focuses forces intuited in the surroundings to not so much calm and order space (as does the classical) as to agitate it and so activate the awareness and actions of citizens. In composition and preferred palette of hard and precise materials (steel and stone), there are affinities with contemporary constructivist sculptors such as Anthony Caro, as well as with some Minimalists. But, because the constructivist approach is generated by context, it is also very close in spirit to site specific sculpture. Though similarities to fashionable deconstructivism are more apparent than real, there are affinities in celebratory programmatic intention with their common source in Russian constructivism.

It is quite fitting then that the first masterpiece of Barcelona's regeneration should be Plaça Sants by Helio Piñón & Albert Viaplana with Enric Miralles. On a concrete deck over railway tracks it juts into a traffic maelstrom, and is less a conventional plaza than a counterpart to the traditional sculptural monument, signifying to those arriving in the city something of its aspirations and cultural glories. And the similarities to contemporary constructivist sculpture suggest affinities to the constructivist era in post-revolutionary Russia – another alliance of socialist politicians and avant-garde artists in a period of recent liberation. Original constructivist art, however, looked forward with

hectoring messages that were blantantly propagandist. Plaça Sants evokes not just the ethereal city of the future but also, with a subtle and sly suggestiveness of surrealism that is so essentially Catalan, conjures resonances with a disappearing past. Though there might be nostalgia for some elements of tradition, the mood is affectionately mischievous rather than sad. Traditional shade elements of pergola and palio are present. While the latter is overscaled and excludes neither sun nor rain, the former undulates as if in an earthquake – freezing perhaps some urgent moment (or explaining the enigmatic absence of conventional elements so unambiguously signified elsewhere). From their size and height, three plinths clearly indicate that each is for one of the traditional forms of portrait statue: bust, standing and equestrian. And from a particular position the fountain seems to cascade down a series of invisible basins.

Piñón and Viaplana's Santa Mònica Museum conversion also employs, besides the constructivist vocabulary of the new elements, surrealist subversions of convention and nostalgic evocations of loss – in this case literally loss of aura. An angled balcony that looks like the Concorde lifting off into the sky at the end of its Ramblas runway raises visitors to the upper level of the old convent (where balconied windows look into subterranean gloom). They then descend again to the ground level cloister. Between two huge arches steel joists slant into the cloister as solid evocations of the shafts of colored sunlight that once slanted down from the stained glass of the demolished church. Despite some exquisite details, particularly the scoring in the external stucco that stops short of openings to suggest absent architraves, and continues as slots across stone shuttered windows, this is a problematic work – an indulgent and undeveloped sketch.

Another constructivist work that evokes missing elements from the past as well as future promise is Enric Miralles and Carme Pinós' conversion of a factory in Badalona into the La Llauna school. Here banks of machine-like ramps and stairs commemorate the original function as well as act as combs channelling and controlling the movement of boisterous schoolchildren. They also provide pulpits for pupils to declaim from as they climb into light from above as well as to enlightenment. An internal dialogue, here between new and old, elsewhere between base and superstructure, is a hallmark of the work of these young architects as part of the way their buildings provoke exploration. For they continue the original constructivist ethos of provoking discovery – of site, setting and self – by literally seeing these from new (shifting and unstable) perspectives.

Plaça Palmera, by architects Pedro Barragán and Bernardo de Solà, dominated by a piece of site-specific sculpture by the American Richard Serra, obviously belongs to this same strand of new work. Though a satisfying project, it is quite without the resonances with the past that add so much to the best of Barcelona's recent architecture.

If the constructivist strand of new architecture tends to make connections to specific aspects of context or the past (often to elements now missing), the classical strand tends to make connections to a more generalized and archetypal past. Esteve Bonell and Francesc Rius' Velodrome and Badalona sports hall projects both elegantly evoke Roman arenas and intense athletic competition as well as Mediterranean archetypes. The Velodrome might also evoke the bullring. If their complete and closed forms evoke little else that is local, both projects nevertheless connect splendidly with their settings as pivots realigning dominant visual axes, thus drawing even distant elements into relationship with them.

If these two buildings retain the pristine, almost archaic, purity of their archetypes, then the work of Bach y Mora welcomes the compromises consistent with our times. Though they evoke classical conventions and codes, they often subvert classical order, playing asymmetry against symmetry, with an equally elegant but lighter and more decorative touch. The sports hall in the Gràcia district is typical of the consistent and pragmatic professionalism of their work, packing considerable volume inside a compact and urbanely composed envelope. The Torre Balldovina school is less understated and more willful in its mannered manipulations of massing.

Bofill, Spain's best known and most successful architect abroad, for a long time had no work in Catalonia. Though his work is classical, his giant orders evoke resonances with only a relatively recent (and non-Spanish) past: with a nineteenth century search for the sublime in a terrifying giantism, and the continuance of this quest in the twentieth century by repressive regimes of left and right. (The buildings and public spaces of his entry for the Olympic Games facilities were all directly and unabashedly derived from Nazi monuments – a puzzling gesture to a newly democratic Spain.) The major virtue of his work lies in its expertise with precast concrete construction. Besides a building for the Olympics, in Barcelona he is now building the National Theater poised as a colossal Greek temple, and the new airport. Though much suppressed behind mirror glass blandness, this is a building that still

belongs to the classical tradition as continued by corporate America. Siting and planning still owe something to the Beaux-Arts, the scale remains gargantuan, and the architectural expression retains lingering vestiges of Mies van der Rohe's Machine Age classicism (at last perhaps a reference to Barcelona, though incredibly oblique), especially as continued by firms like Roche, Dinkeloo and Associates.

Very different from this and in no way classical, is the hotel complex by Moneo and Manuel de Solà-Morales. It is situated on Diagonal, which steps up at either end in plan and elevation to be as wedded to its setting as the Auditorium is aloof from its site. More exuberant than these two and also on Diagonal is a hotel by Carlos Ferrater, which might owe something to deconstructivism as well as Portman and perhaps Coderch. Though part of the private sector, hotels belong in this book because their facilities enhance the public life of a city.

Even though so many of Barcelona's best new buildings tend towards the constructivist or classical, there are of course other ways to relate to context and history, some demonstrated by extensions to existing monuments. Oscar Tusquets' refurbishment and extensions of Domènech i Montaner's Palau de la Música attempts a sympathetically turreted massing and vegetal decorative detail. In antithesis, Ignasi de Solà-Morales' extensions to the Liceu Theatre make no attempt to compete with the original, but are modestly understated, abstracting and continuing the proportions and rhythms of the existing building. His additions though are so extensive that a more expressive approach might have overwhelmed the original building, while Tusquets' relatively smaller extension had to be able to stand up to the original building. Particularly satisfying at the Palau de la Música is the new seating by Tusquets – but then product design is the field that has occupied him most in recent years.

Yet another approach to interventions in old buildings is demonstrated by Josep Llinàs at the Archaeological Museum. The virtue of this is that he has followed the logic of the existing building and the new program so consistently that though it lacks nothing in character, nobody would say the work was characteristic of Llinàs. In contrast, the insertions by Gae Aulenti at the Palau Nacional are in willful opposition to the spirit and logic of the building. It can only be hoped that this time this strategy proves more successful than her work at Paris' Musée d'Orsay.

Other additions to the public realm are engineering works that in their uncompromised form owe nothing to history, and yet should prove to be landmark monuments that will soon be intrinsic to the identity and memory of the city. Such works are Norman Foster's Communications Tower and Santiago Calatrava's Felip II bridge. The latter looks splendid in photographs, but in its dinky scale and no longer pristine whiteness it is in reality a little preposterous. It makes sense though when understood as not just a functional installation but as a gem ornamenting the city. Calatrava's gantries supporting traffic lights on Diagonal seem better judged in the match of scale and sculptural expressiveness. They are contemporary counterparts to the Art Nouveau lights on the Passeig de Gràcia, and so have precise resonances with the city. They exemplify then what is best in the recent architecture of Barcelona.

# The Olympic Village

# Nova Icària

## Josep Martorell

**1.** As part of its municipal planning policy of transforming the physical environment of the city by means of projects in key urban spaces, in 1985 the Barcelona City Council decided on a new objective: the large-scale transformation of a sector of the city through the creation of a new maritime district.

The industrial area of Poble Nou, between the Ciutadella Park and the Avinguda d'Icària – which used to be called "the Catalan Manchester" on account of the magnitude of its industrial output – was segregated from the rest of the city and cut off from the sea by the railway line running from França Station. The obsolescence into which the area had fallen, and its state of urban degradation, extremely difficult to upgrade or restore, called for its total transformation. Narcís Serra had the felicitous idea of proposing a new neighborhood for the Olympic Village, following the decision to put Barcelona forward as a candidate for the 1992 Olympic Games. Pasqual Maragall, Serra's successor and Mayor of Barcelona since 1982, has been the great champion of the project, managing to put it in action and giving it worldwide credibility.

**2.** The project, begun at a time when it was still not known whether Barcelona would host the 1992 Olympics, was entrusted to the architects Martorell/Bohigas/Mackay/Puigdomènech. The fundamental question was one of giving the neighborhood a new and central character, transforming its capacity for use, form and representative character, accessibility and network of facilities. Coincidentally, this would be the Olympic Village during the 1992 Olympic Games. Then from 1993 on, it would be a maritime neighborhood integrated with the complex realities of Barcelona.

**3.** An analysis of the successive parallel strips of land, not juxtaposed but completely interconnected, which make up the neighborhood from seafront to interior, will allow for a global understanding of the urban design proposal.

**3.1.** A system of beaches, structured around the breakwaters which protect the storm water outfall pipes running into the sea, and a small harbor in the center of the Nova Icària sector, constituted the specific Olympic requirements, which will convert the harbor to the port for light sailing events, and subsequently to a leisure port.

**3.2.** A pedestrian seafront esplanade, running alongside the beaches and the port, and understood as an extension of the present Passeig Marítim in the Barceloneta. With the transformation of the harbor into the Olympic port, the Passeig Marítim has been divided into two separate stretches: one in the Barceloneta and one in Poble Nou.

**3.3.** The Avinguda del Litoral, as part of the peripheral ring road system running along the coast, has been designed as a great park-cum-thoroughfare, constructed in its entirety within the bounds of the Olympic Village. This park-thoroughfare picks up vehicles in two lateral traffic lanes: one on the landward side, rectilinear and aligned with the Cerdà grid; one on the seaward side, sinuous and following the sinusoidal line of the new beaches. In the middle is a great park (197 feet wide at its narrowest point), the Parc del Litoral, with high-speed through traffic segregated and routed beneath it. Its course and its subdivided section mean that this does not constitute an obstacle to movement between city and beach, and serves to connect it with the orthogonal grid of the Cerdà Eixample.

**3.4.** A series of free-standing buildings, among them the two skyscrapers which flank the Passeig de Carles I. These will not create a visual barrier for the city, since the complex of complementary buildings, low in height, will give the Passeig Marítim and the Olympic port a continuous facade and serve as a stimulus to urban activity along the seafront. This activity will be reinforced by Barcelona's first line of residential urban facades immediately overlooking the sea, with a continuous portico on the ground floor facing the landward side of the Avinguda del Litoral.

**3.5.** The genuinely residential neighborhood, planned as a continuation of the traditional 19th century fabric of the Eixample, already laid out in this sector to a greater or lesser extent. This will, nevertheless, set out to resolve one of the crucial problems in the reconstruction or planning of new neighborhoods: the preservation of traditional urban morphology at the same time as the employment of modern residential typologies which make for improved living conditions. To this end, the superblock structure was adopted, in which the line of the perimeter follows the traditional form of the city – with the buildings aligned along the street – while there is room for greater autonomy in the articulation of the interior spaces, allowing the use of typologies not found in the historic city centre.

It must be pointed out that one of the basic ideas of the urban planning scheme provides the entire complex with a backbone of landscaped public spaces of considerable dimensions, the design of which should provide the basis for the unity and global identity of the new neighborhood. The vertebral elements are: the Carles I Park, which meets up with the extension to the Ciutadella Park; the Bogatell pedestrian walkway, which crosses the district diagonally, already in existence as a result of the construction of the great stormwater drainage system; a park which runs through the interiors of the blocks in the north-east of the area (formerly the Torras factory) from the junction of the Avinguda del Bogatell and the Passeig de Carles I; the complex of parks and esplanades alongside the beaches and the Avinguda del Litoral; the Litoral Park, the Passeig Marítim of Poble Nou and the Poble Nou Park. With these public spaces, moreover, the absolute coherence of the entire road network for the sector can be maintained.

**4.** In order to guarantee the formal outcome of the architectonic and urban design operation, yet without infringing on the individual creative scope of the architects and engineers who would subsequently be involved, an approach or method was developed and applied through a set of four documents: an explanation of the criteria governing architectural formalization, an exemplary design sketch, a graphic presentation of quantities and a number of building regulations. Of the fundamental criteria, the following are of particular relevance:

**4.1.** Division of the complex as a whole into thirty-four Project Units, grouped together in nine Superunits. Each of these Units, to be entrusted to a different architectural team, was described separately in the four documents and conceived of as a single project. The great axes defining the public space were also approached as Project Units.

**4.2.** A typological repertoire, suggested in the design sketch, which was intended to ensure the conceptual direction of the architectonic form.

**5.** The move from design project to action was made at the end of 1986. The municipal company Vila Olímpica, S.A. (VOSA) initiated the process of acquiring land, building the infrastructure and recovering the beach. The architects Martorell-Bohigas-Mackay-Puigdomènech who designed the project, were called on to work in collaboration with VOSA, and Josep Martorell joined the management team to direct and coordinate, with the architect Juli Laviña, the urban design and architectural aspects of the operation.

However, the global project still needed to take new steps in the process of elaborating definitive solutions in both architectonic and urban design terms. Without this intermediary step it would have been impossible to move on from the initial stage to that of the projects for the buildings. This involved determining, on a larger scale, the volumetric and architectonic character of the building, and incorporating the morphological and typological transformations which were to enrich the initial schemes, together with most recent data on the infrastructure projects, the Olympic uses, and the social and functional hypotheses for the post-Olympic period. At this stage the architects Jaume Bach, Gabriel Mora, Roser Amadó, Lluís Domènech, Esteve Bonell and Francesc Rius became involved, their work complementing that of the designers of the project.

**6.** The next stage was the drawing up of projects for the public buildings and spaces. For the residential area, the designation of architects was made on the initiative of the municipal authorities. On the basis of objective criteria, and independent of the local administration, all those architects who had won a FAD (Foment de les Arts Decoratives) Architecture award in the past thirty years were invited to participate. The architects entrusted with the various different project units were the following:

5.1   Mitjans/Ribas Piera
5.2   Godia/Urgell De la Villa
5.4   Cantallops
5.6   Compta/Arañó/Mora
5.8   Sanmartí
5.9   Bonet Castellana/Klein/Scarpato
5.10  Taller de Arquitectura (Ricardo Bofill)
5.11  Giráldez/Subias/López
6.1/6.2  Martorell/Bohigas/Mackay/Puigdomènech
7.1   Llimona/Ruiz Vallès
7.2   Correa/Milá
7.4   Puig Torner
7.5   Clotet
7.7   Anglada/Gelabert/Ribas
      Tusquets/Díaz & Assoc.
      Valls/Mateos/Benedito
8.1/8.7  Bonell/Rius/Gil
8.2   Viaplana/Piñón
8.3/8.4  Bosch/Tarrús/Vives
8.5   Alemany/Poblet/Cirici
8.6   Martínez Lapeña/Torres

The global project also contains five gateway buildings, which give continuity to the line of the facades of the superblocks. These are independent elements, and it was decided, in view of their dimensions and form, that they should be offices, and that their development should be put up for public tender. The architects of the buildings are Bach/Mora, Amadó/Domènech, and Viaplana/Piñón, the last named responsible for three of the five buildings.

7.   The port of Nova Icària is one of the most significant public spaces in the new maritime neighborhood of Barcelona. It did not exist in the 1986 project. Its forerunner was a small circular harbor which came into being as a consequence of the need for a hard urban space between the two beaches, Somorrostro and Nova Icària, which would allow the arcs of these beaches to be kept within manageable limits. The harbor, treated as a marine piazza, invited the siting of a conference centre on one of its sides, a building which would serve to explain the meeting of the Passeig de Carles I with the sea.

The need to create a base for Olympic sailing competitions made it necessary to expand the area of water landwards and to the east. The port of Nova Icària, with its breakwater in the shape of a great arc 1640 feet long and stepped in section, with complete control over the form, is the result of close collaboration between Joan Ramon de Clascà, the engineer responsible for infrastructure at VOSA, and the Martorell-Bohigas-Mackay-Puigdomènech team of architects.

Olympic requirements also called for quays much larger in area than those of any leisure port. This will provide, after the 1992 Games, a great public space by the sea for leisure uses, surrounded by shops, restaurants, and the site of a future municipal sailing school with its own boatyard.

8.   The buildings which will bring the port area to life are: a hi-rise hotel with a complementary building occupied by shops, restaurants and leisure facilities, by Bruce Graham (SOM), Frank Gehry and Josep Juanpere; an office tower by Ortiz/León, and a building for the Catalan meteorological service and offices for the Ministerio de Obras Públicas y Urbanismo (MOPU) by Alvaro Siza Vieira and Joan Falgueras.

In the port itself, just by the harbor mouth, the conference center by José Antonio Martínez Lapeña and Elías Torres will stand at the end of the Passeig de Carles I.

9.   In the residential area of the Olympic Village, projects for two parks, a monumental fountain and two public service buildings were made the subject of competitions.

The Carles I Park is a fundamental element in the organization of the space connecting the new neighborhood with the city, conceived as an extension to the Ciutadella Park, it is a response to the curving lines of the perimeter of Ciutadella, and those of the buildings which mark the entrance to the Olympic Village from the Passeig de Carles I. The winner of the competition was the architect Josep Zazurca.

The competition for the Poble Nou Park, between the old neighborhood, opposite the Rambla Avenue and the sea, which contains the training track for athletes during the Games, was won by the architects Xavier Vendrell and Manuel Ruisánchez, with their intelligently devised landscape of dunes.

The competition for the monumental fountain at the junction of the Passeig de Carles I and the Avinguda del Litoral was won by the architect José M. Mercé's minimalist project.

The competition for the multipurpose sports complex was won by the architect Juan Navarro Baldeweg, who proposed a very adroit compositional solution. However, due to problems quite unconnected with Baldeweg, the scheme to be constructed is that by architects Franc Fernández, Moisés Gallego and Pep Soler, competition finalists, which effectively and soberly resolves the program and the building's integration into the Cerdà-style chamfered corner of the site.

The competition for the school building and fire station was won by the architect Yago Conde. The site has been changed since the competition, but the adaptation of the original scheme to the new setting has been resolved with great clarity.

The Litoral Park, within which the coastal bypass road is contained, is a project by Martorell-Bohigas-Mackay-Puigdomènech, one of the essential significative elements of the overal urban design proposal.

## Francesc Mitjans

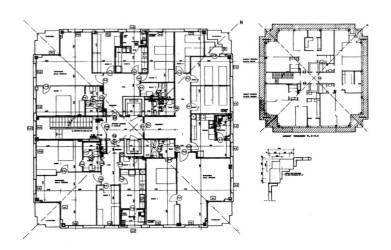

## Manuel Ribas Piera

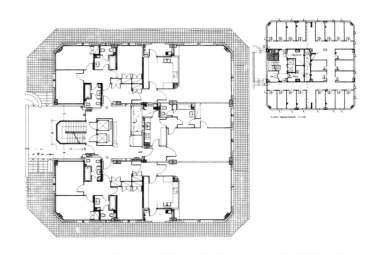

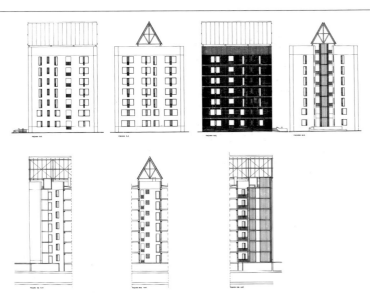

## Manuel Sergi Godia/Josep Urgell/María Pilar de la Villa

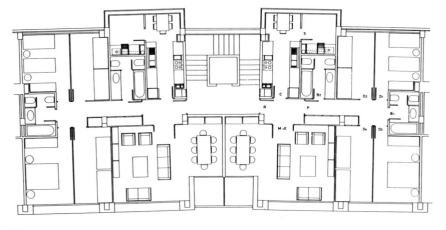

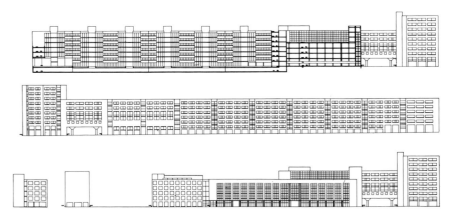

Lluís Cantallops/Miquel Simón

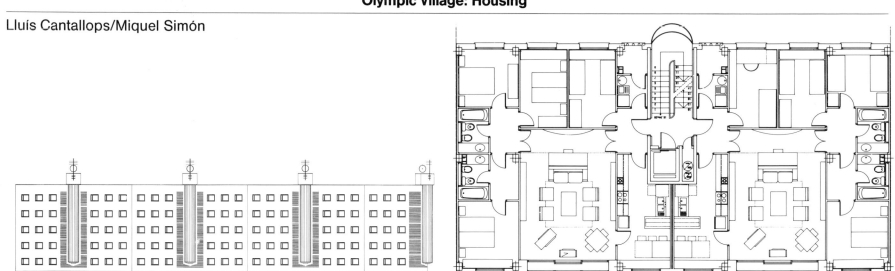

Ernesto Compta/Claudio Arañó

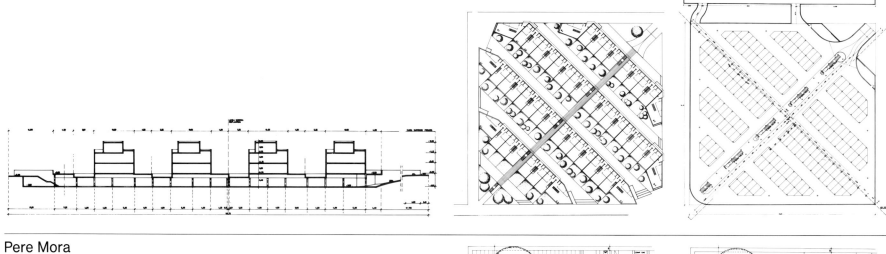

Pere Mora

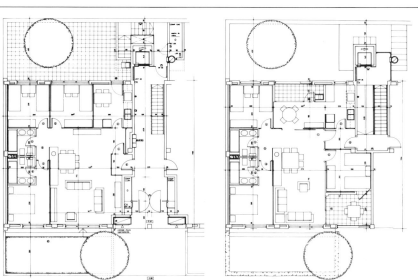

## Jaume Sanmarti

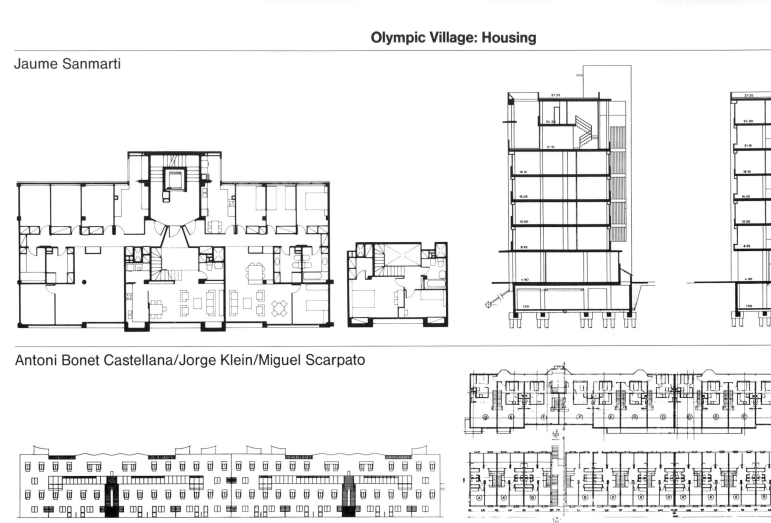

## Antoni Bonet Castellana/Jorge Klein/Miguel Scarpato

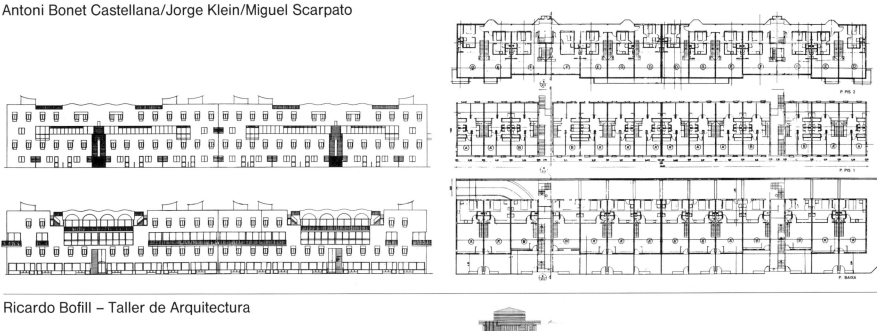

## Ricardo Bofill – Taller de Arquitectura

Guillem Giráldez/Xavier Subías/Pere López

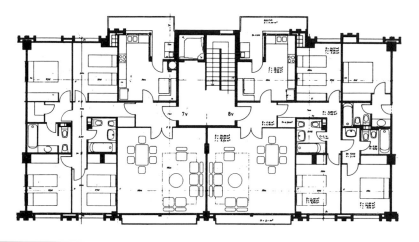

Josep Martorell/Oriol Bohigas/David Mackay/Albert Puigdomènech

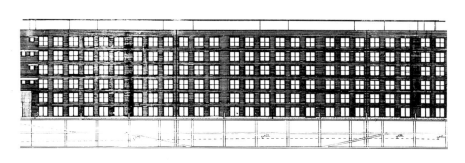

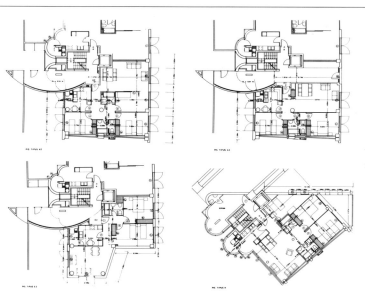

Pere Llimona/Xavier Ruiz Vallès

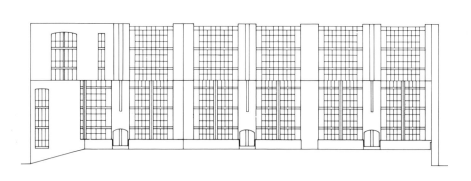

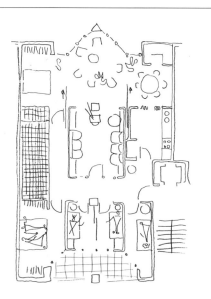

Federico Correa/Alfonso Milà

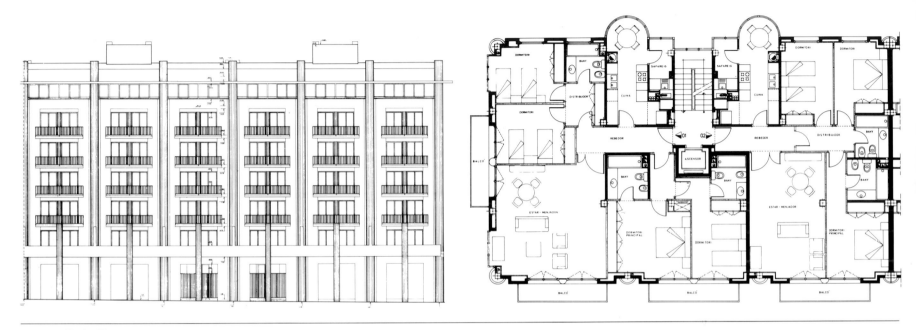

Josep Puig Torner

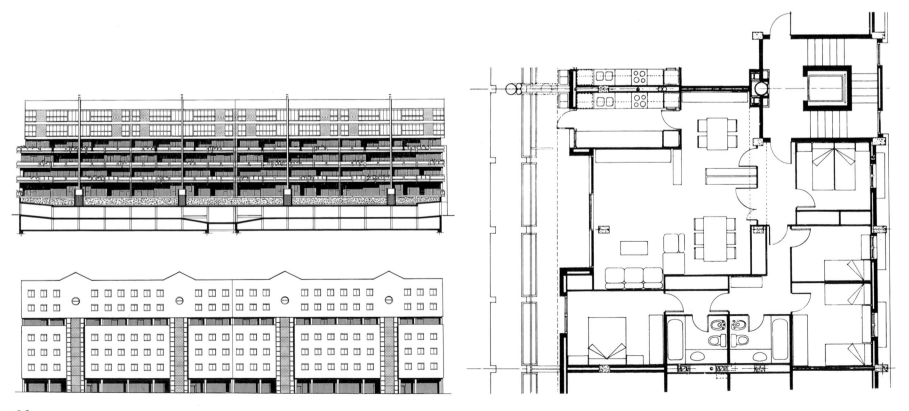

Lluís Clotet/Ignacio Paricio

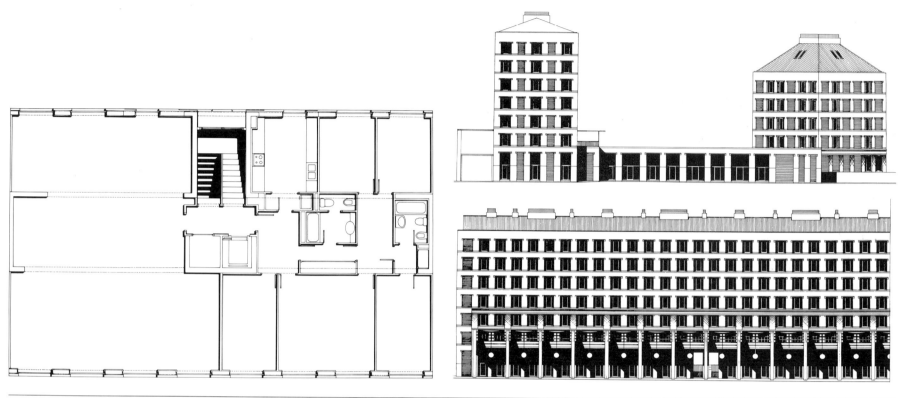

Esteve Bonell/Francesc Rius/Josep Maria Gil

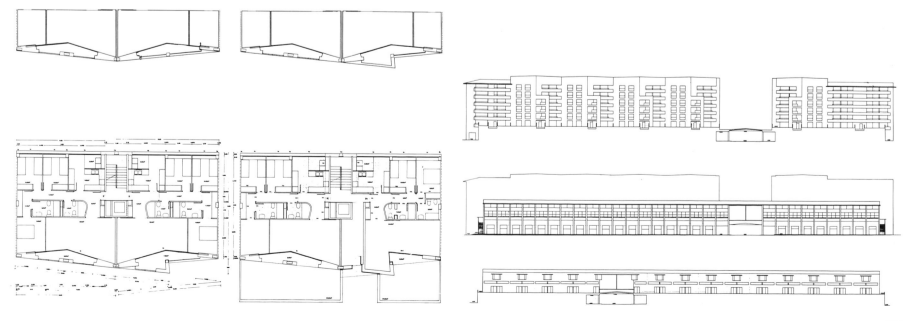

Albert Viaplana/Helio Piñón

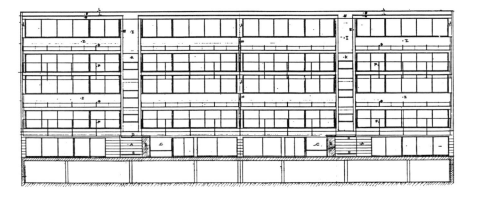

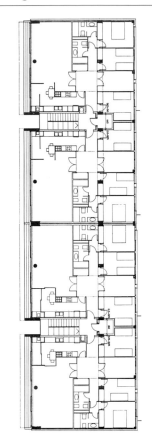

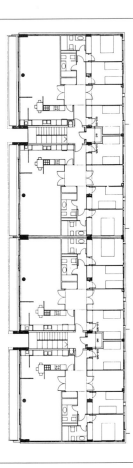

Jordi Bosch/Joan Tarrús/Santiago Vives

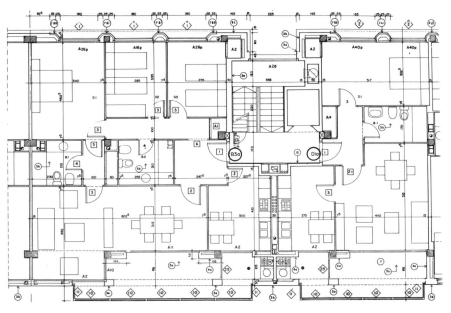

Josep Alemany/Enric Poble/Jordi Cirici

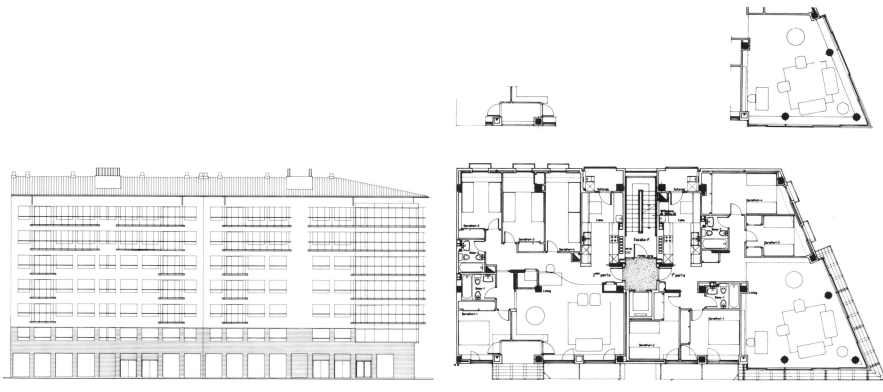

José Anntonio Martínez Lapeña/Elías Torres

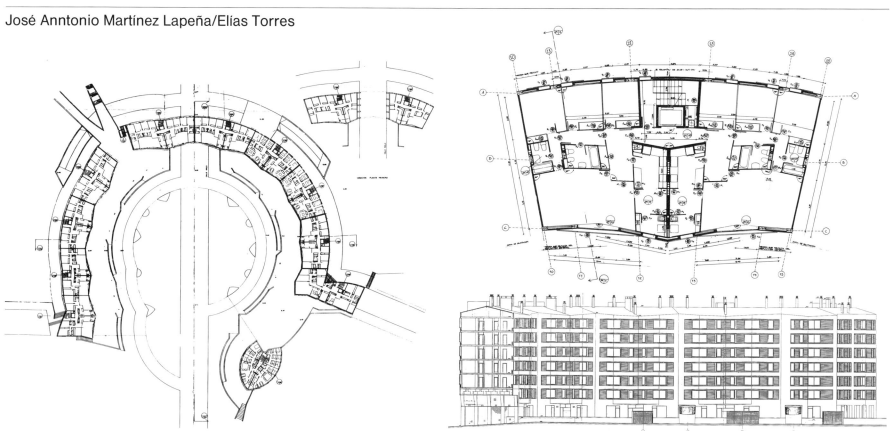

Tusquets/Díaz & Assoc.
Oscar Tusquets/Carlos Díaz/Andrés Monzú

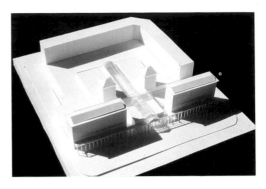

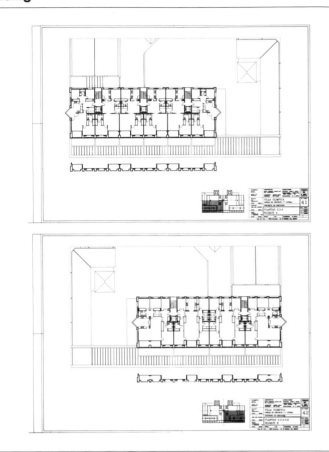

Ramón Valls/Agustí Mateos/Josep Benedito

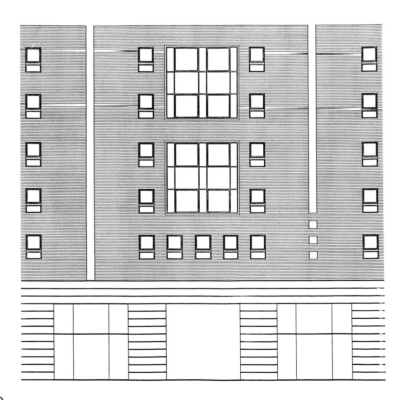

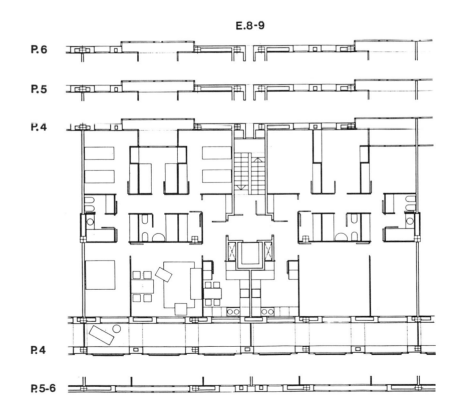

Carlos Ferrater

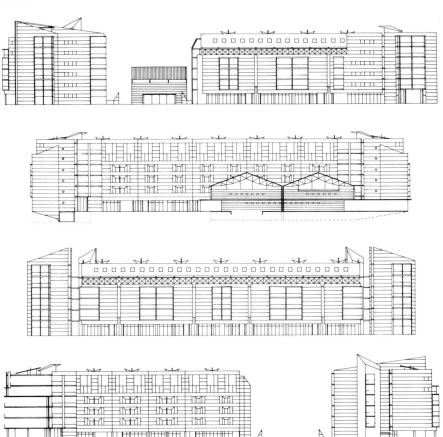

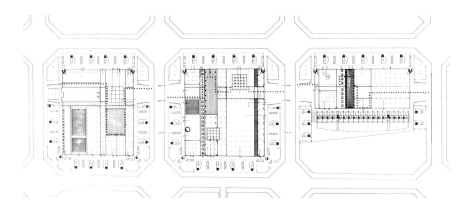

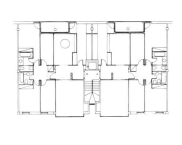

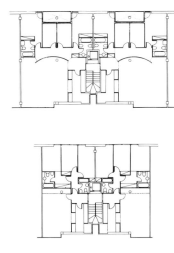

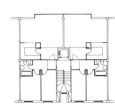

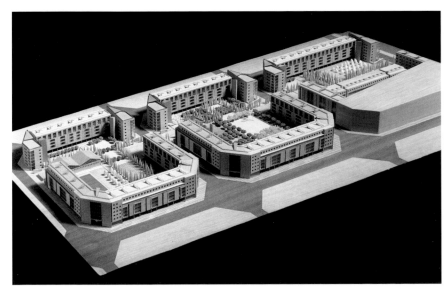

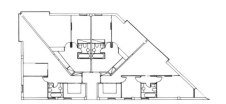

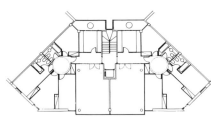

Roser Amadó/Lluís Domènech

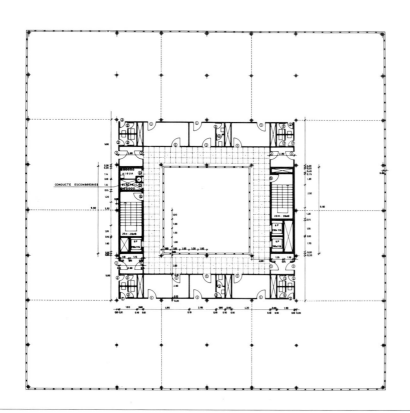

Jaume Bach/Gabriel Mora

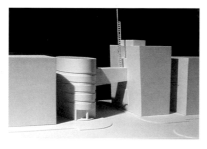

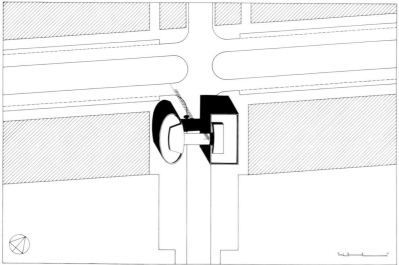

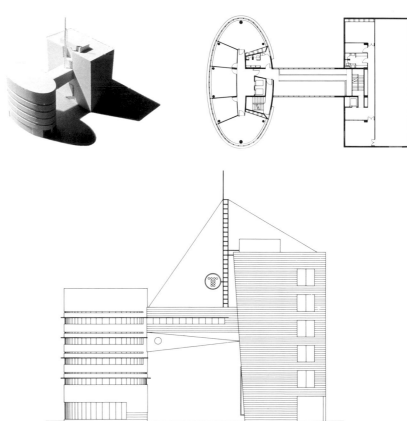

Albert Viaplana/Helio Piñón

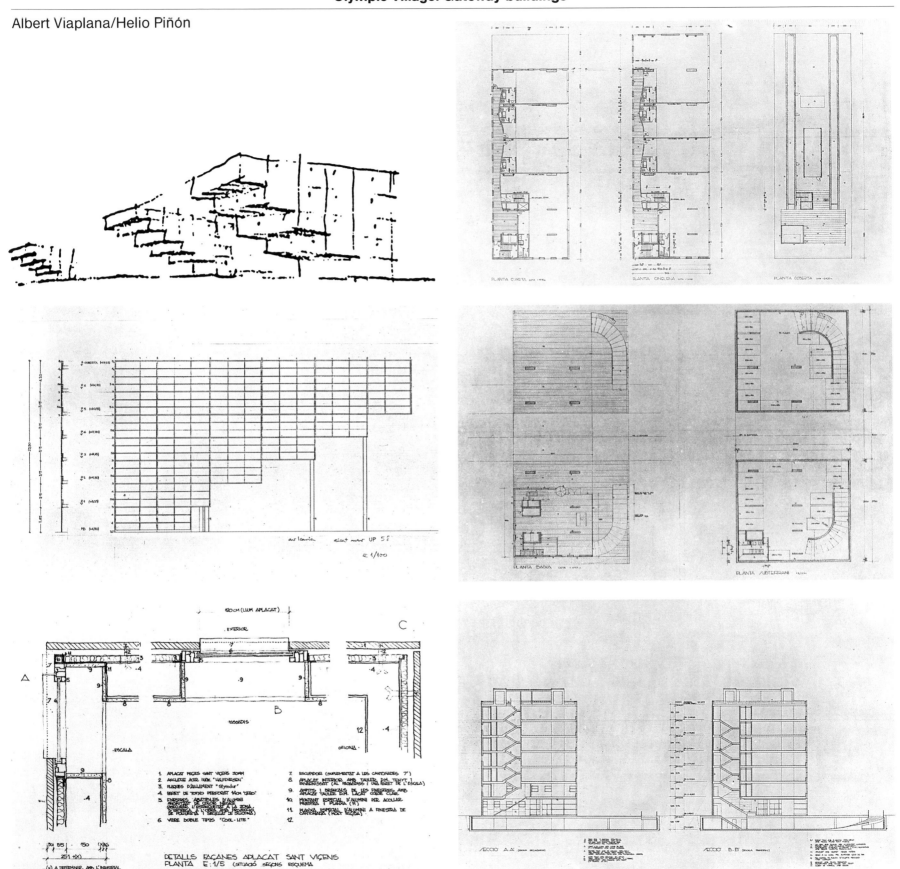

Litoral Park
Josep Martorell/Oriol Bohigas/David Mackay/Albert
Puigdomènech

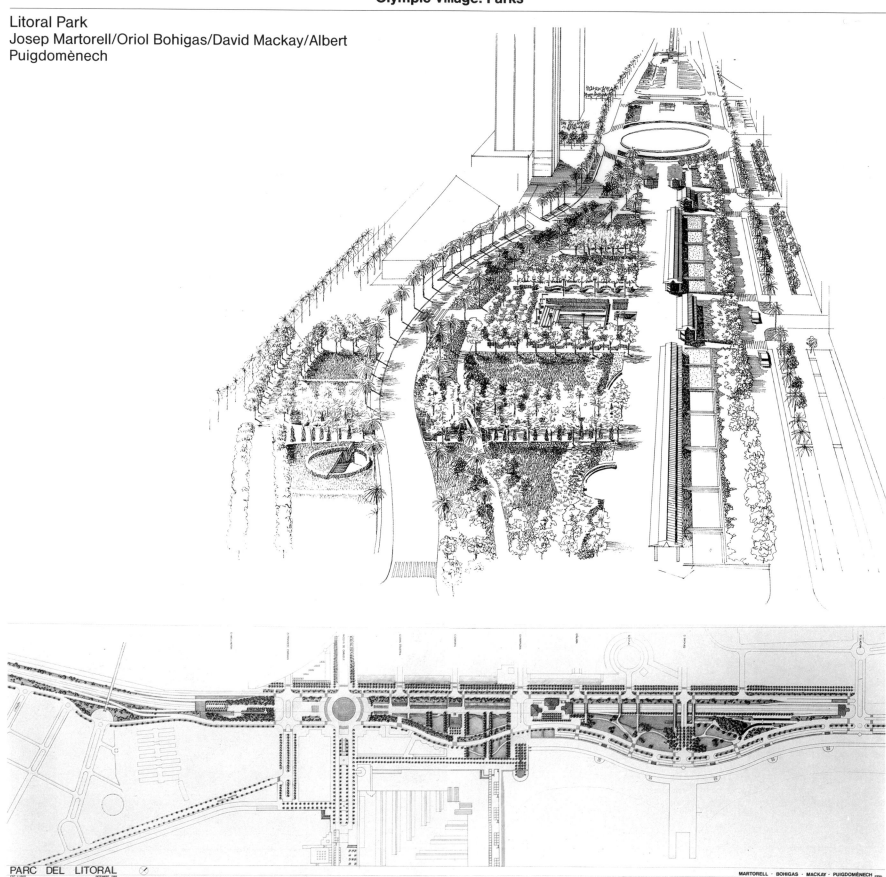

PARC DEL LITORAL

MARTORELL · BOHIGAS · MACKAY · PUIGDOMÈNECH

Poble Nou Park
Manuel Ruisánchez/Xavier Vendrell

Carles I Park
Josep Zazurca/Mariona Muixart (assistant)

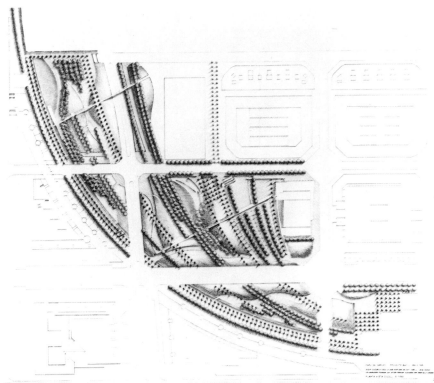

First Aid Center
Manuel Sergi Godia/Josep Urgell/María Pilar de la Villa

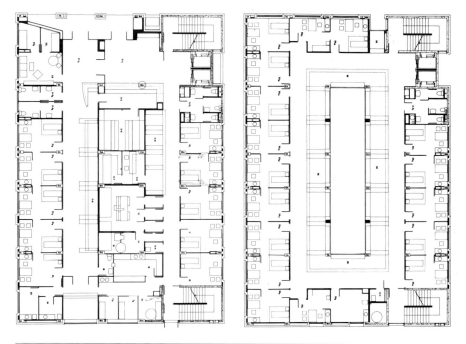

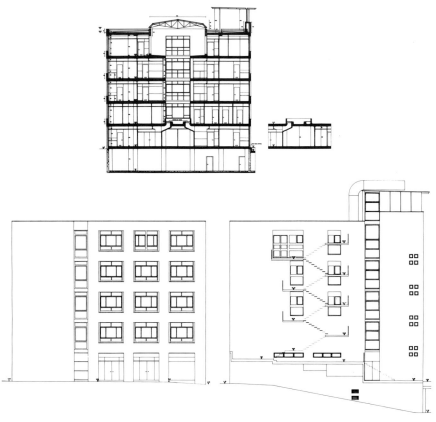

Sports pavillion
Franc Fernández/Moisés Gallego/Pep Soler

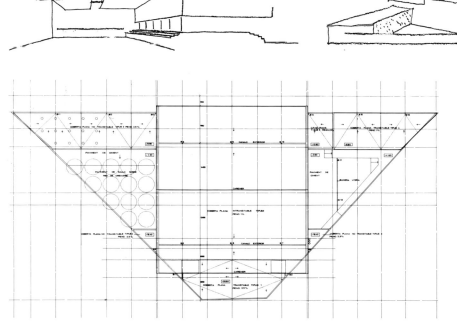

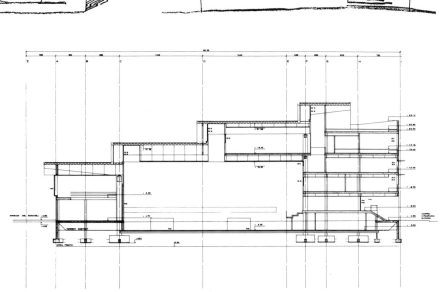

Monumental fountain
J. M. Mercé Hospital

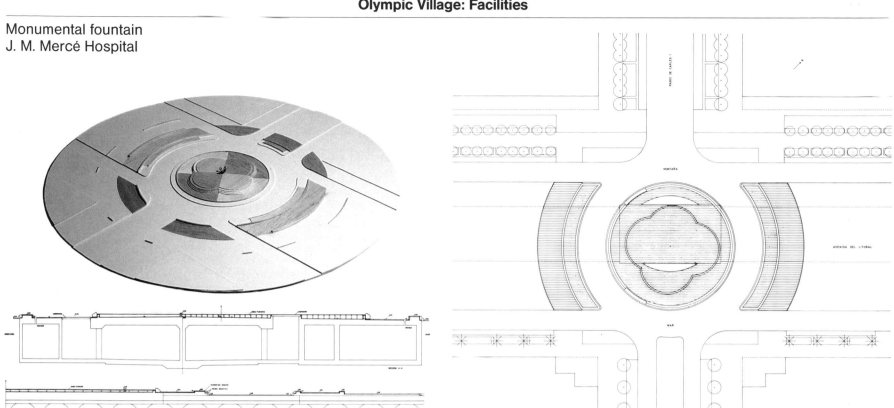

School and fire station
Yago Conde

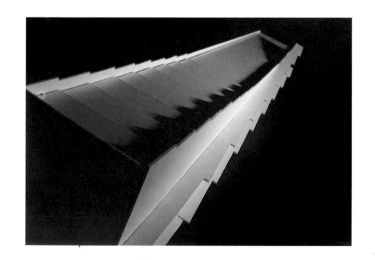

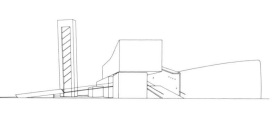

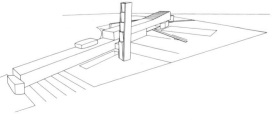

MOPU building and meteorological center
Alvaro Siza Vieira/Joan Falgueras

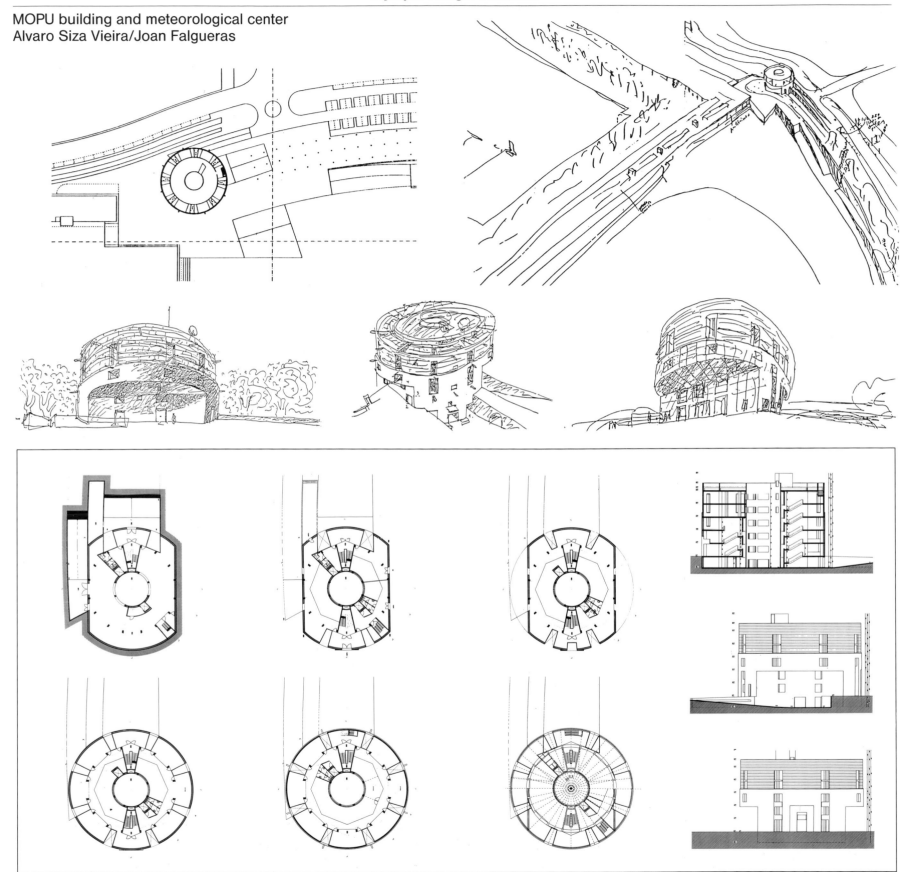

Conference Center
José Antonio Martínez Lapeña/Elías Torres

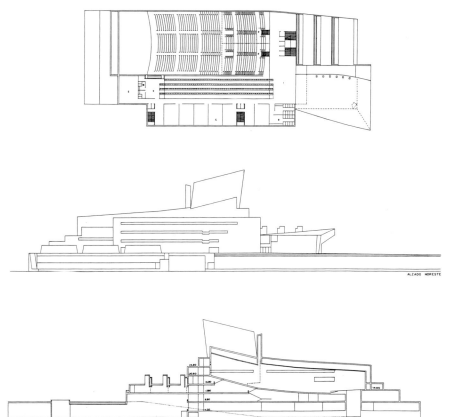

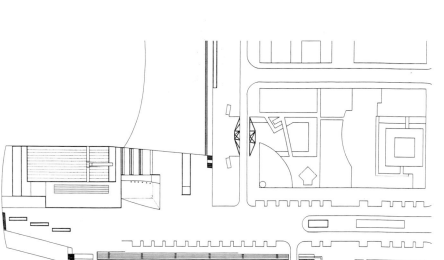

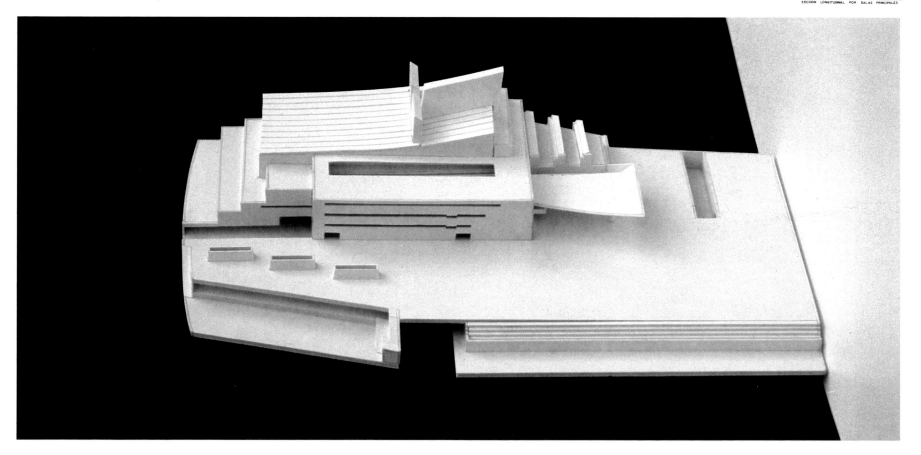

## Olympic Port

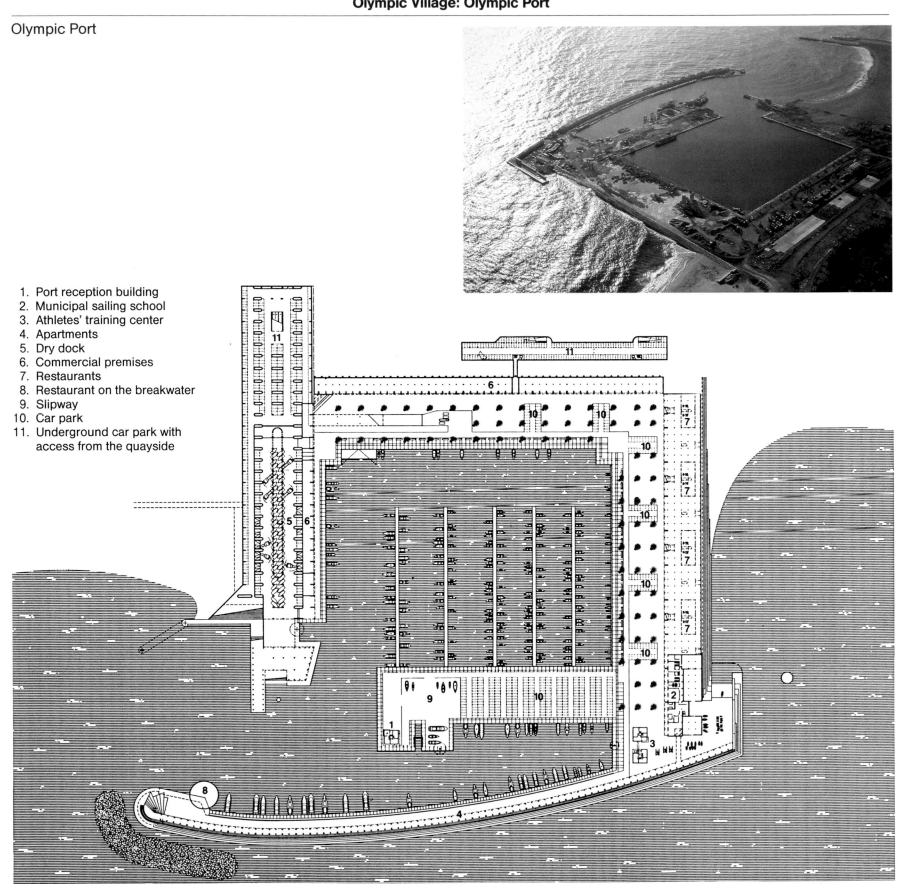

1. Port reception building
2. Municipal sailing school
3. Athletes' training center
4. Apartments
5. Dry dock
6. Commercial premises
7. Restaurants
8. Restaurant on the breakwater
9. Slipway
10. Car park
11. Underground car park with access from the quayside

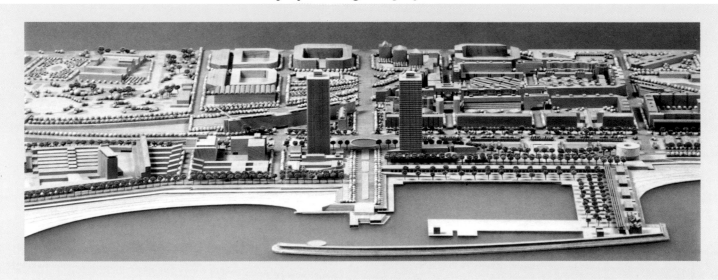

# MAPFRE office building
## Iñigo Ortiz/Enrique León

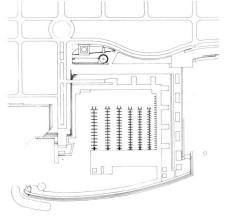

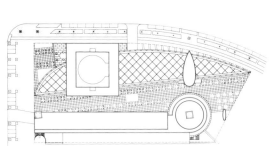

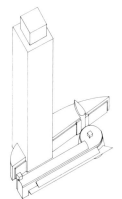

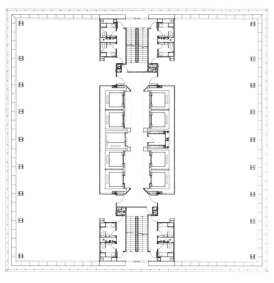

Vila Olímpica Hotel
S.O.M./G.C.A.

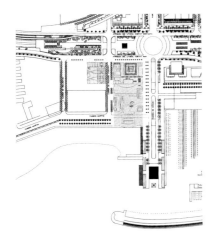

# Sports facilities

Remodelling of the Olympic stadium

Sant Jordi sports pavilion

National Institute of Physical Education of Catalonia (I.N.E.F.C.)

Badalona municipal sports pavilion

La Teixonera tennis club

Municipal sports pavilion and pelota complex, in Vall d'Hebron

Horta velodrome

Gràcia sports complex

Architects: Federico Correa/Alfonso Milá/
Carles Buxadé/Joan Margarit/Vittorio Gregotti

Assistants: Spartaco Azzola, Josep Gómez, Victòria Alavedra,
Carme Costa, Valèria Datzira, Anna Cabrera, Joan Deulofeu,
Ramon Ferrando, Pepa Gómez, Ramon Llobera, Josep Llinàs,
Àngels Negre, Josep Sala, Joan Torrelló, Fina Royo, Artur Puig,
Miquel Poch, Lluís Marcos, Concha Mateo,
Carme Mas, Andrés Lezcano

# Remodelling of the Olympic stadium

## Montjuïc, Barcelona    1986-1989

The presence of collective memory and emotion on the hill of Montjuïc is symbolized, in the Olympic area, by the stadium building, the great sports construction of the 1929 International Exhibition.

The desire to respect symbol prompted the conservation of the building's image, standing as it does at the highest point on the Olympic esplanade, which slopes gently down from the terrace opposite the stadium's west facade to the level of the Hidráulica, a distance of some 2 300 feet.

The concept of the intervention retains the existing appearance of the stadium while it achieves the necessary improvements in comfort, services, communications and aesthetics. Attention was therefore focussed primarily on adapting the building to increase its functional capacity, while still retaining the original appearance.

The main facades, and the dimensions which these facades impose on the floor area, are the basic constituents of the image mentioned above, and these were considered unalterable in the approach to this project for the Olympic stadium which, in view of its capacity and general characteristics, is to host the opening ceremony of the '92 Olympics.

The adaptation of the stadium to meet present-day needs made it necessary to expand the seating area. This was achieved by sinking the competition area deeper and thus extending the lower part of the stands.

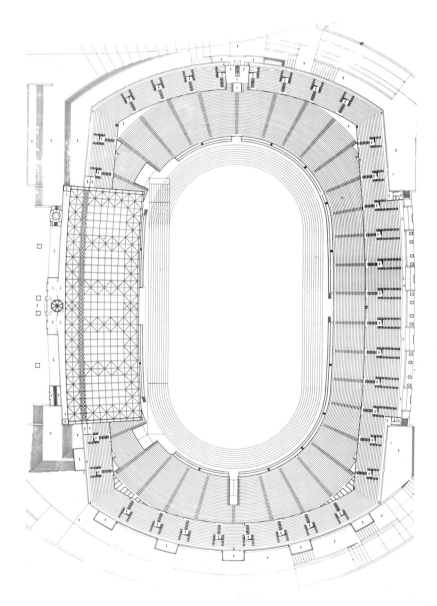

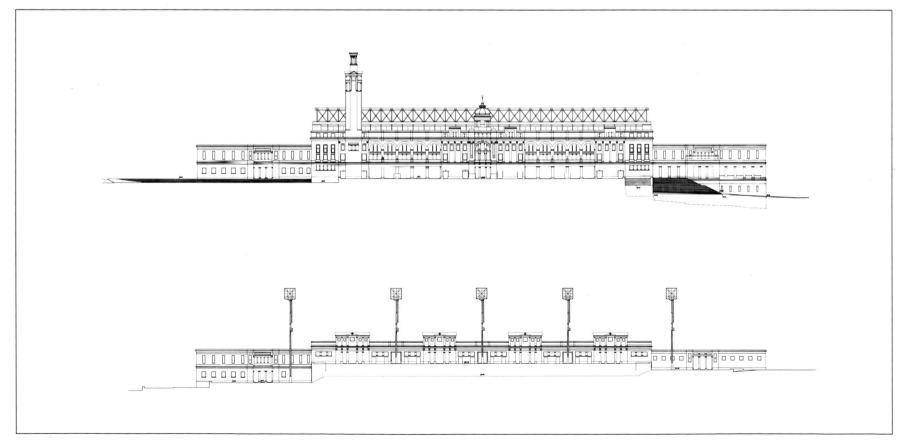

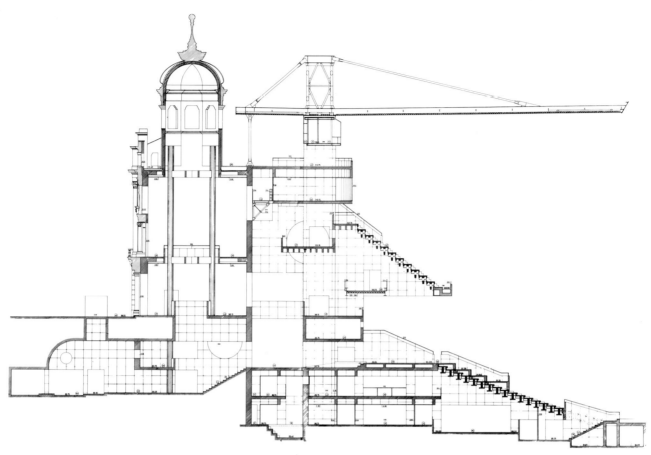

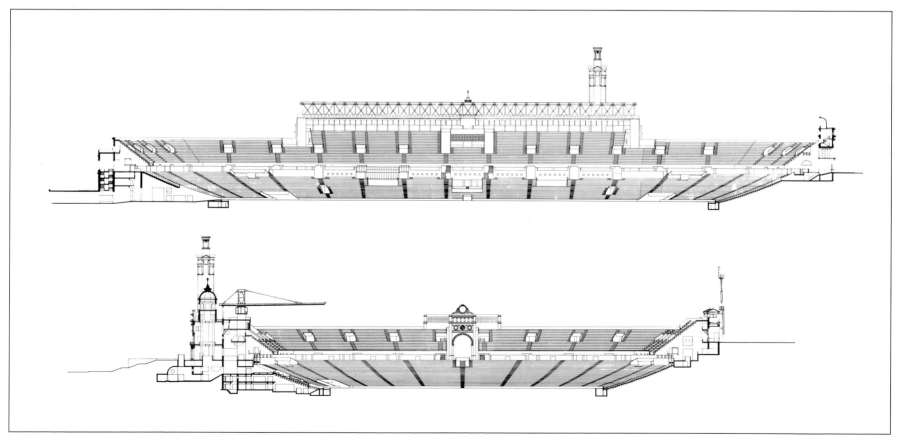

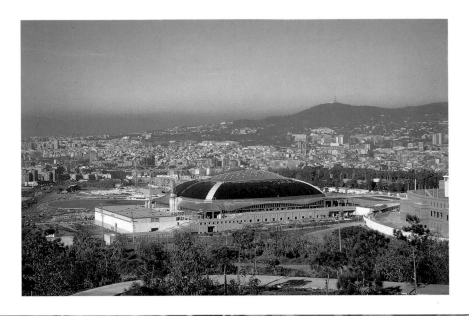

Architect: Arata Isozaki

Site architects: Rafael Delgado, Esperanza Estefanell

Assistants: Shuichi Fujie, Juan Carlos Cardenal,
Hiroshi Aoki, Naoki Inagawa, Shogo Kishida, Masato Hori,
Kunio Usugi, Fernando Álvarez, David Correa, Emil Palou,
Eva Serra, Rafael Villasante

Coordination: Toshiaki Tange, Akiko Okabe

# Sant Jordi sports pavilion

## Montjuïc, Barcelona    1984-1990

The functional and structural conception of the San Jordi sports
pavilion is based on two fundamental spaces, each of which
corresponds to a competition area.

The larger of these, the so-called Palau Principal, with capacity for
17,000 seated spectators, is covered by a great cupola conceived and
resolved by means of a spatial structure which is supported on its
perimeter.

The other space, the multipurpose Pavelló Polivalent, is based on a
rectangular floor plan which can be subdivided into four sports areas
by means of a system of partition curtains incorporated into the design
of the roof of the pavilion, a single flat metal structure which covers the
entire space.

Between these two pavilions is another construction which will be used
for a variety of functions, and three courtyards for ventilation and
illumination. This central volume houses the greater part of the services
for the complex.

The Palau Principal has direct access from the great square of the
Olympic Ring. The multipurpose Pavelló Polivalent can be considered
as auxiliary to the great hall for major events, without impeding its
being used independently on a regular basis, since it also has direct
access from the exterior by way of two footbridges on the Palau's east
and west facades. The program is developed over a series of different
floors, which take their names from the height of the level they occupy.

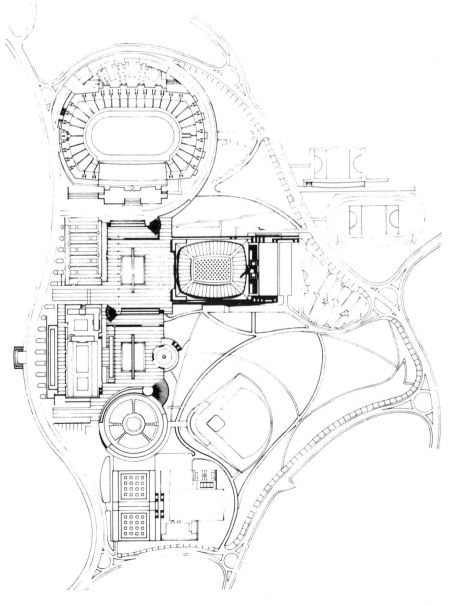

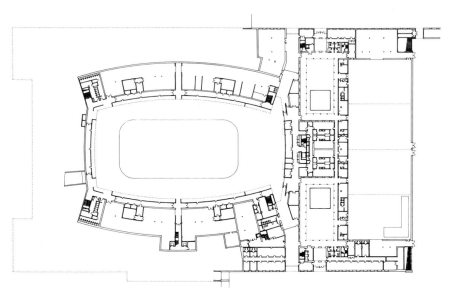
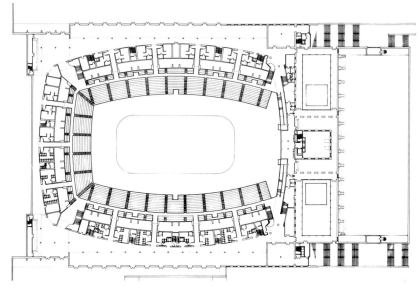

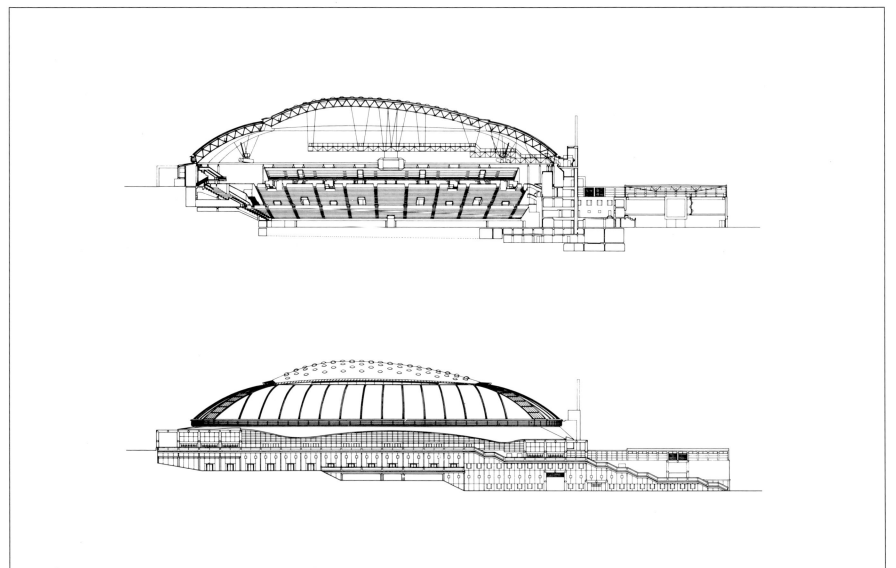

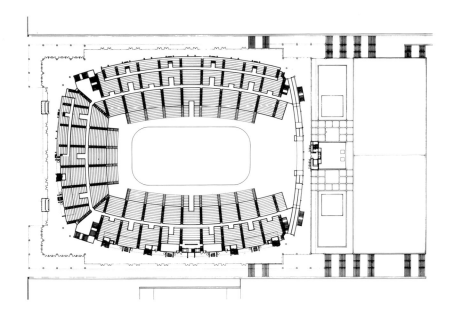

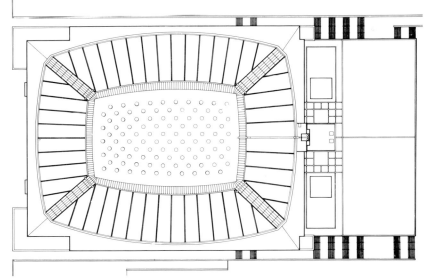

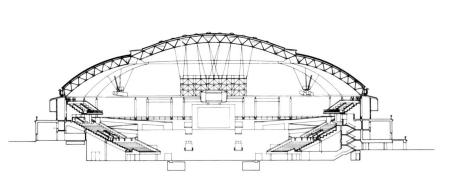

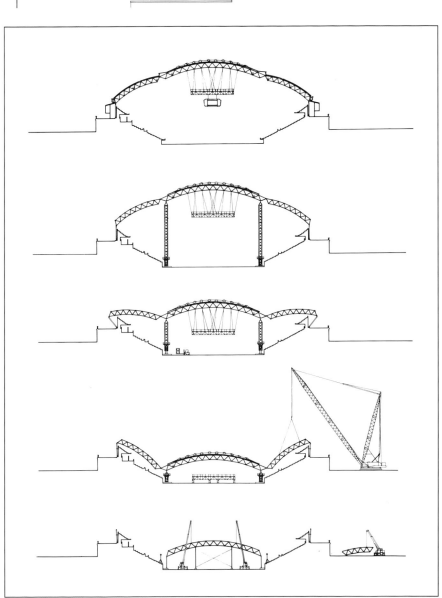

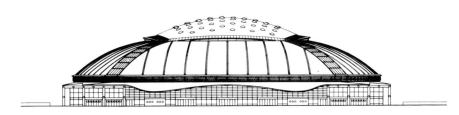

Architect: Ricardo Bofill – Taller de Arquitectura

Assistants: Peter Hodgkinson, Patrick Genard,
J. M. Rocías, P. Messecke

Structures: INYPSA

# National Institute of Physical Education of Catalonia (I.N.E.F.C.)

## Montjuïc, Barcelona    1984-1990

This building, situated within the Olympic Ring on the hill of Montjuïc, is to house the I.N.E.F.C. physical education institute, in addition to accomodating a variety of sports events and serving as the press center during the 1992 Olympic Games.

The building's configuration, which draws on the typology of the cloister, is easy to read: two buildings set down around a courtyard and linked together by an arcade.

The architectonic language, classical in inspiration, has been simplified to the maximum. The use of architectural concrete (a precast system), combined with the treated aluminium and smoked glass of the fittings, give the building a sober, composed modernism, with the result that the whole integrates harmoniously with the general context of the hill and the gardens.

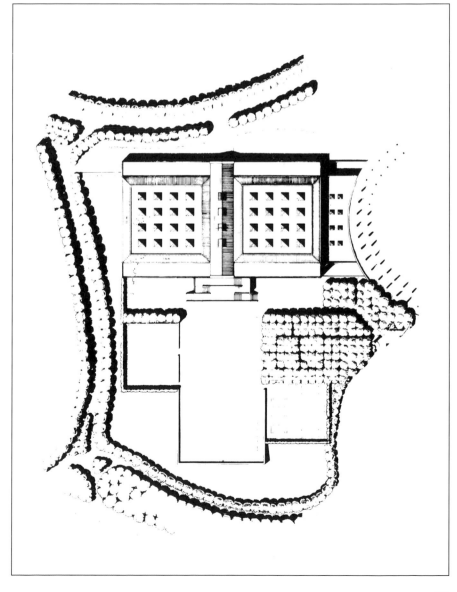

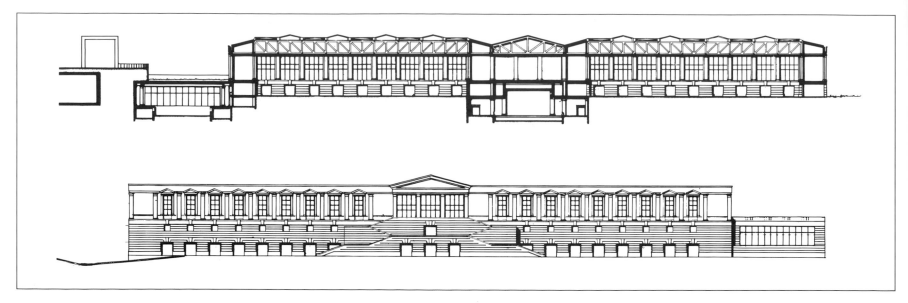

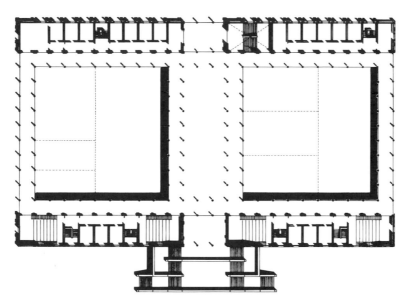

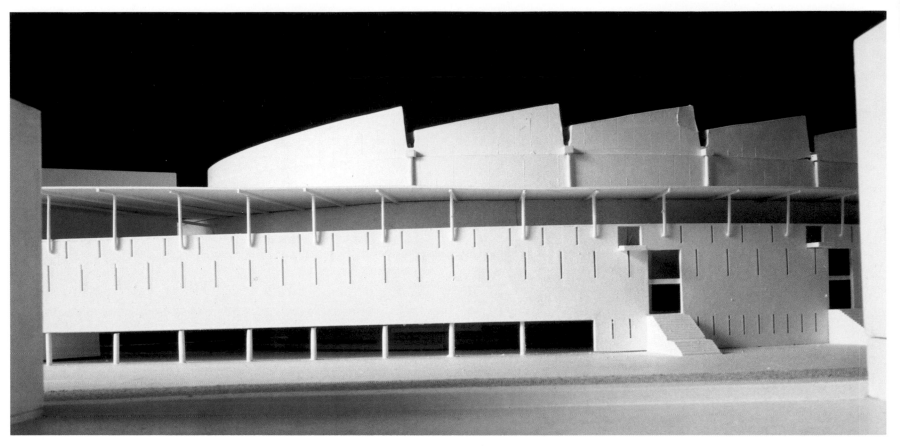

Architects: Esteve Bonell/Francesc Rius

Assistants: Desirée Mas, Marie-Christine Aubry,
Jaume Calsapeu, Enrique Rego, Pere Rius

Structures: Robert Brufau, Agustí Obiols,
Lluís Moya (architects)

# Municipal sports pavilion

## Badalona, Barcelona    1988-1991

A sports pavilion raises three fundamental isues:

1.  The functional and programmatic proposals.
2.  The connection with a prefigured urban structure which conditions the building, and the urban tension which the building sets up with its surroundings.
3.  The question of the roof, a factor exclusive to this type of building.

The common denominator of these three points is their large scale. We are talking here about a building with a capacity for twelve thousand spectators; a building 492 feet long and 328 feet wide. A symbolic and representative building to which the concept of a "cathedral of sport" might well be applied, in the sense of its being the principal site for a particular activity – in this case the playing and watching of top level netball events.

The concept of the cathedral is synonymous with that of a great roofed space which marks the final point of an urban procession, in which the spectator arrives after a series of spaces, at a place where emotions will be aroused by scale, proportion and light.

This is a space with a meaning of its own, quite apart from the spectacle which unfolds within it. When in use, it becomes a single, unitary space in which both spectators and players unquestionably form part of the spectacle, and where each person is the unit of measurement of the grandeur of the space.

The outcome is an extremely precise building, simple in spite of its great size, displaying great autonomy of form. At the same time it inserts itself into the urban context, ordering and giving significance to a particular situation within the city.

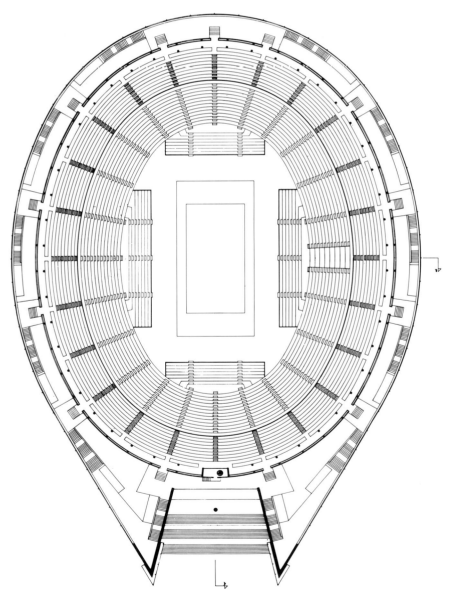

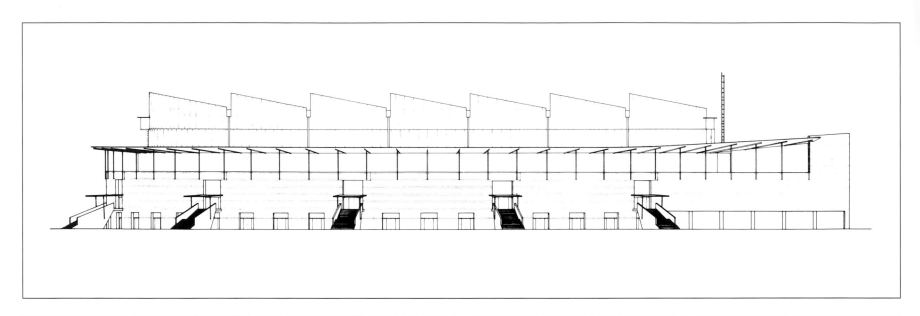

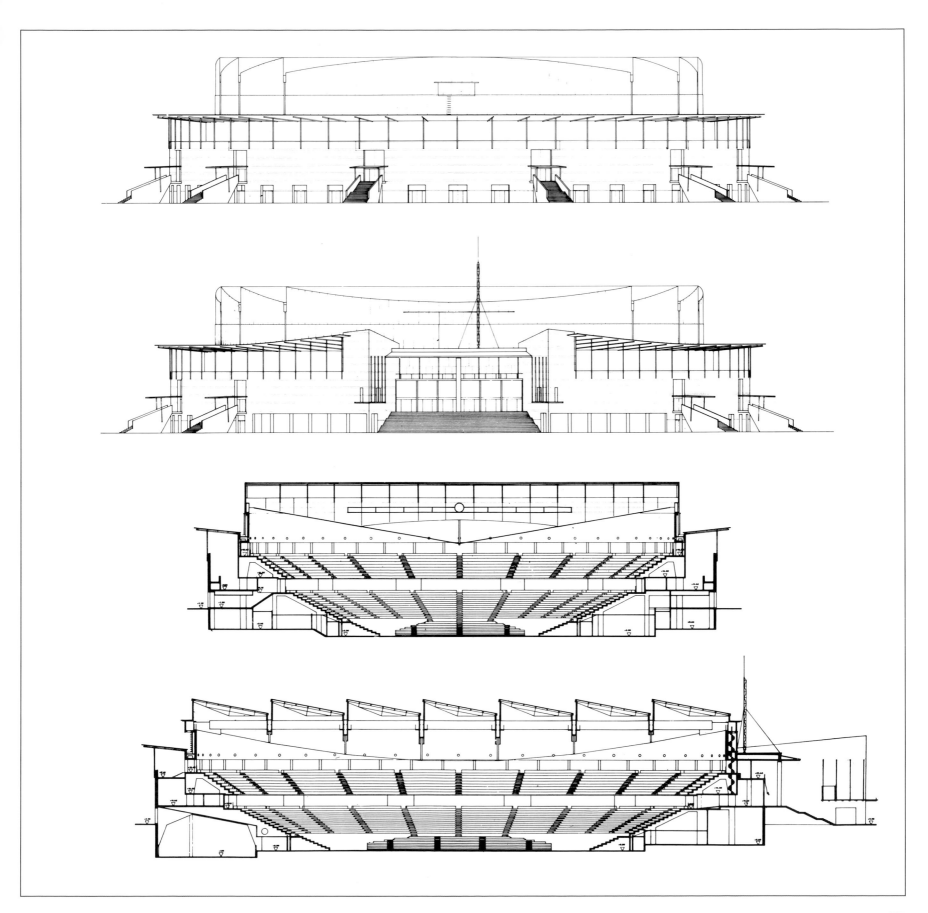

Architect: Tonet Sunyer

# La Teixonera tennis club

## Vall d'Hebron, Barcelona   1990-1991

The program for this sports complex devoted to tennis includes a social club, a central court with capacity for ten thousand spectators, and an additional sixteen courts, some for training and some for lower-level competitions.

The original topography of the site was diagonally traversed by a large watercourse. Given the incompatibility of this feature with the laying out of a tennis complex, the scheme started from an artificial topography ordered over a series of terraces. These terraces are stepped down from west to east.

Situated on the Vall d'Hebron, on the first terrace, to the west, the scheme envisages a large triangular access area and car park for VIPs and competitors.

The second terrace is some 30 feet below the first, coinciding with the ground floor of the building, which is buried under the first terrace, extending linearly for 427 feet, with access at either end.

The central court is set like a great crater, excavated out of the middle of this second platform. This leaves two large areas to the sides for the evacuation of the spectators, which at the same time makes it possible to expand the capacity to ten thousand seats.

From this point on, the remaining twelve courts are laid out on terraces with a difference in level of 3.94 feet. This difference in level has been used to provide each court with three tiers of seating. The complex as a whole is organized like a city, in which the courts are the blocks to be served and the corridors between them the access streets.

Finally, a more pronounced difference in level makes way for two indoor tennis courts, a fronton court, and a landscaped area in which a last court sits, asking to be read in the manner of a rectangle of beaten earth in the midst of a garden.

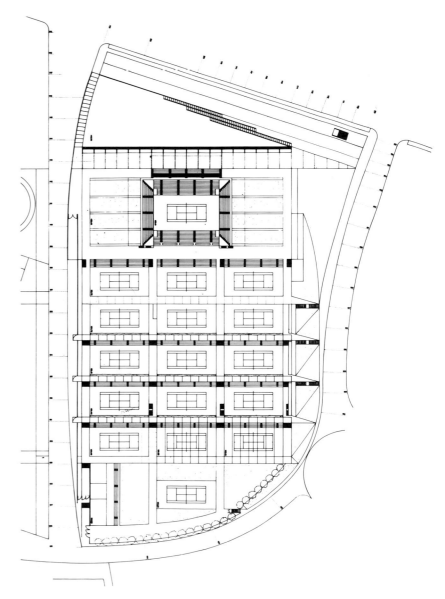

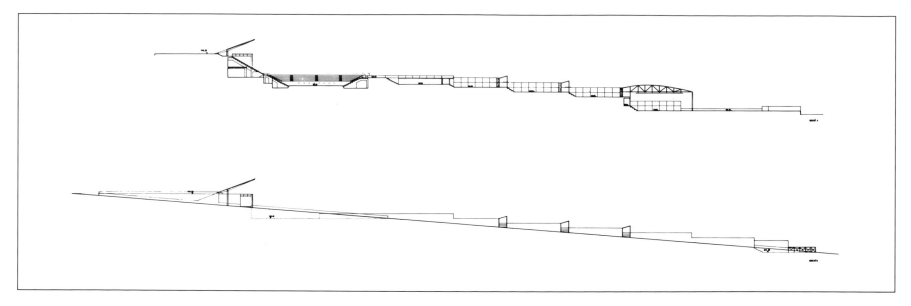

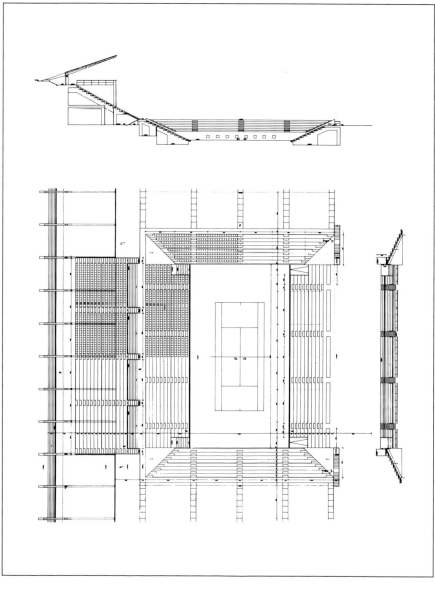

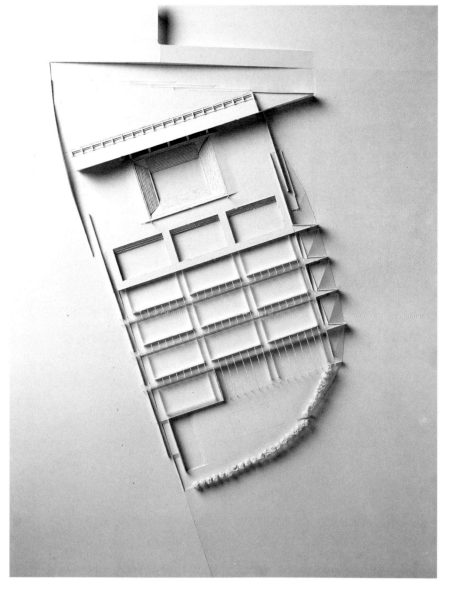

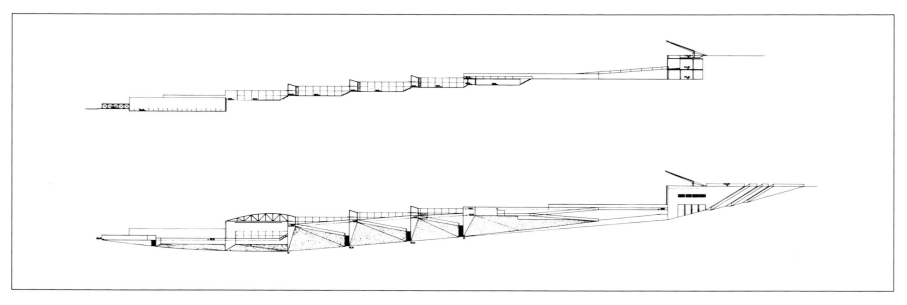

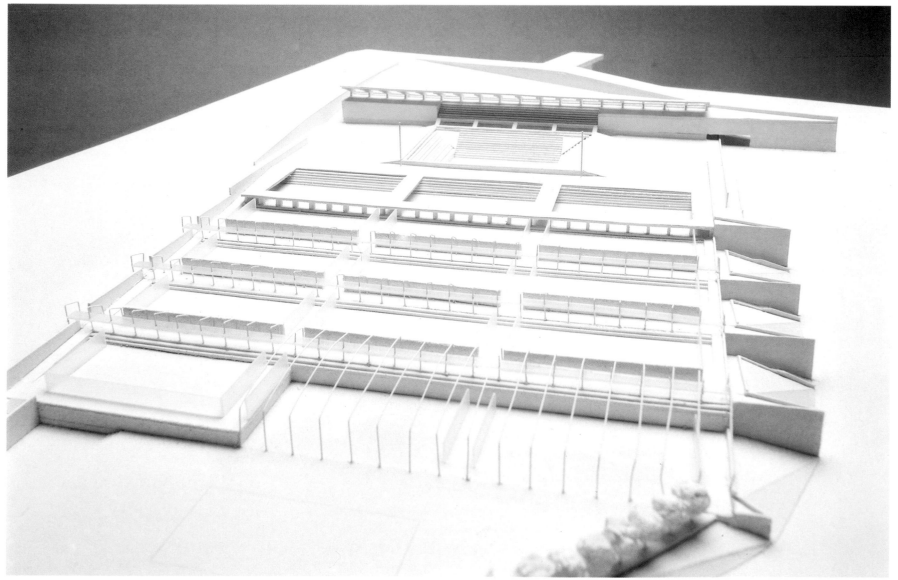

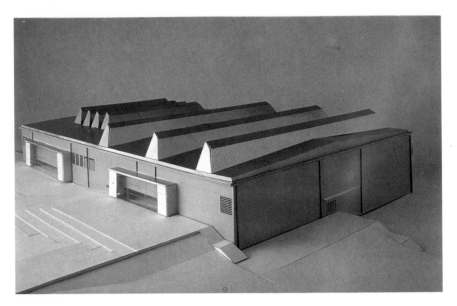

Architects: Jordi Garcés/Enric Sòria

Assistants: Rafael Soto, architect, Estudio BGM

Structures: Joan Margarit, Carles Buxadé, architects

# Municipal sports pavilion and pelota complex

**Vall d'Hebron, Barcelona   1989-1991**

The typology chosen for this project is the outcome of inscribing the extremely diverse physical and organizational parameters needed within the simplest and spatially clearest volume possible, in the interests of achieving optimum results in the correct scaling of the sports halls and in the order of their relative positions.

The facades, of exposed brick, contribute to the abstract character of the complex, having been conceived as immense curtains perforated by the ordered sequence of openings generated in the interior.

The roof, metallic and essentially flat, with projecting north-facing skylights, takes the leading role in a building of these proportions, standing on a predominantly sloping site.

The total built area is 190,177 square feet, with a capacity of 4,608 spectators.

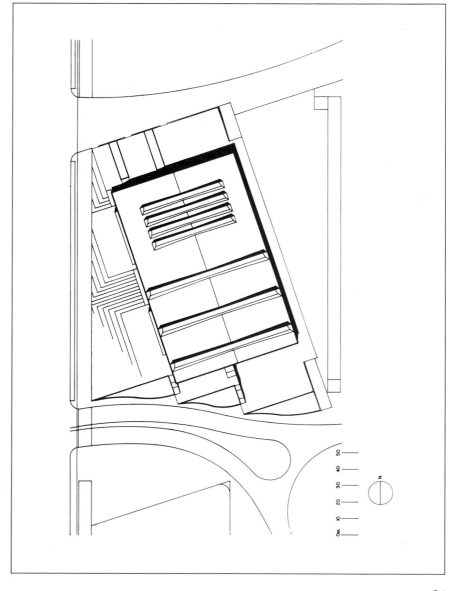

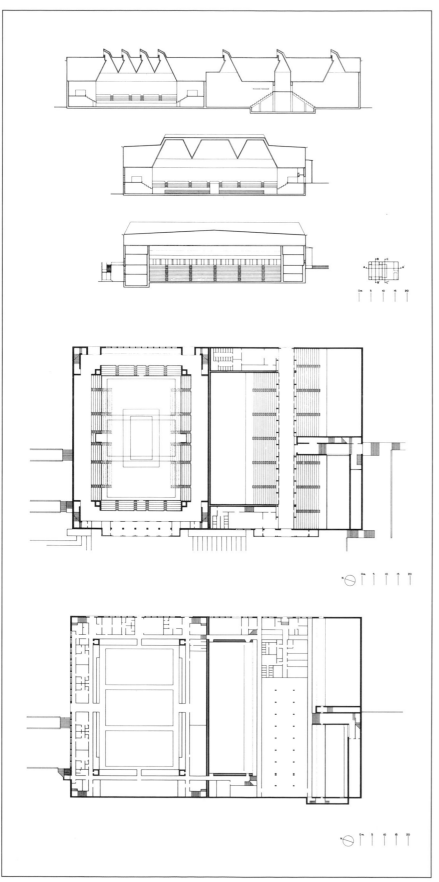

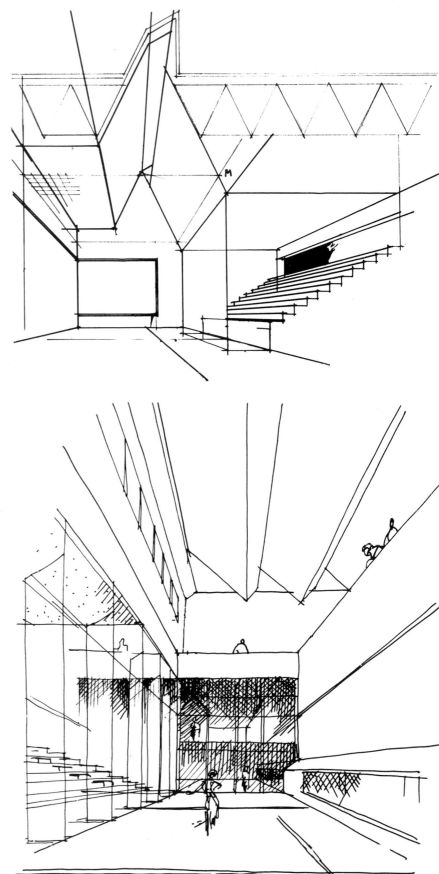

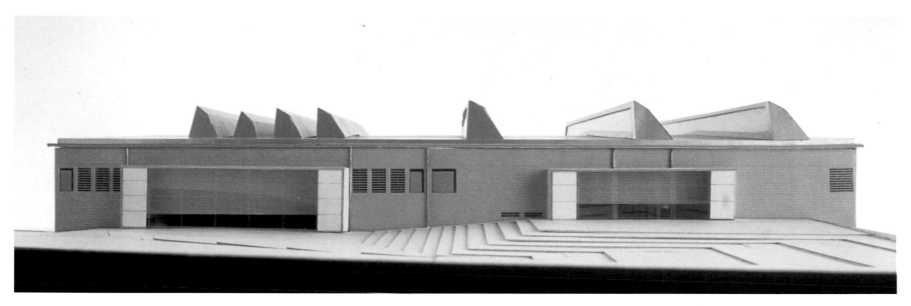

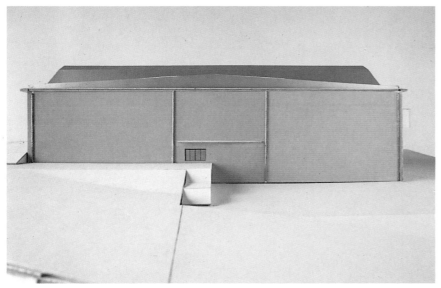
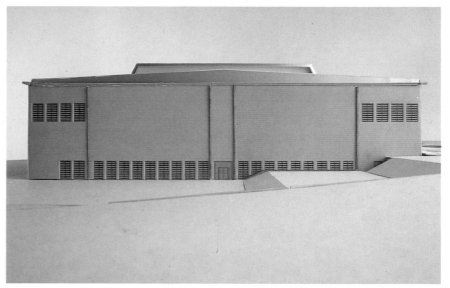

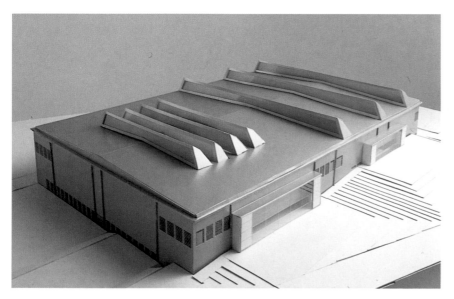
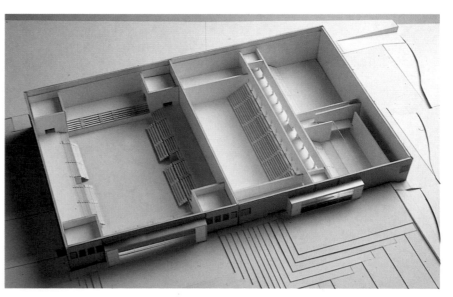

Architects: Esteve Bonell/Francesc Rius

Assistant: Herbert Shurman

Structures: Robert Brufau, architect

Sculpture (visual poem): Joan Brossa

# Horta velodrome

## Horta, Barcelona    1982-1984

The location here was a plot with no real definition of its own, which made the siting of the building extremely difficult. The problem lay in the positioning of a construction of very little programmatic complexity but considerable area in plan. The result was a building which would accomodate itself to the site with a certain fluidity, which in spite of its dimensions would be supported by the terrain, and be as transparent as possible; a building conceived on two scales, one distant, one close up. At the same time, what was desired was a building with a clear image which would define itself as an architectural unit, and be capable of exercising an organizing influence on its immediate surroundings as a whole.

The idea of the *rotonda* allowed for a plan with a continuous facade, which would present itself uniformly to the different external circumstances which the building would have to confront. The circular perimeter wall serves to order the geometries of the interior space, and provide for the construction of a dome as a possible means of roofing the interior.

The velodrome has a certain classical quality as well as a developed modernism: classical in its manner of situating itself in the landscape, and in the rotundity of its conception; modern in its pragmatic and realistic aspects, in its simplicity and the way the construction is appropriate to the materials used.

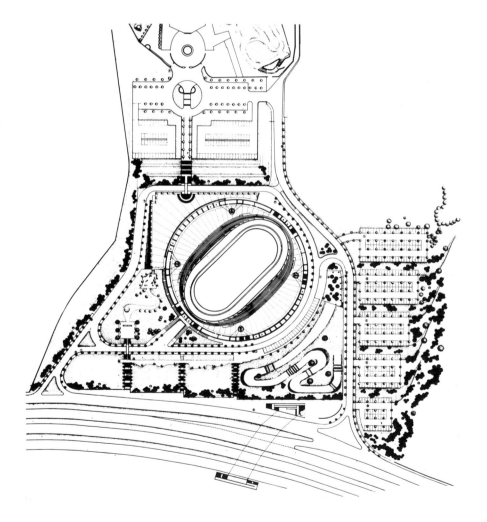

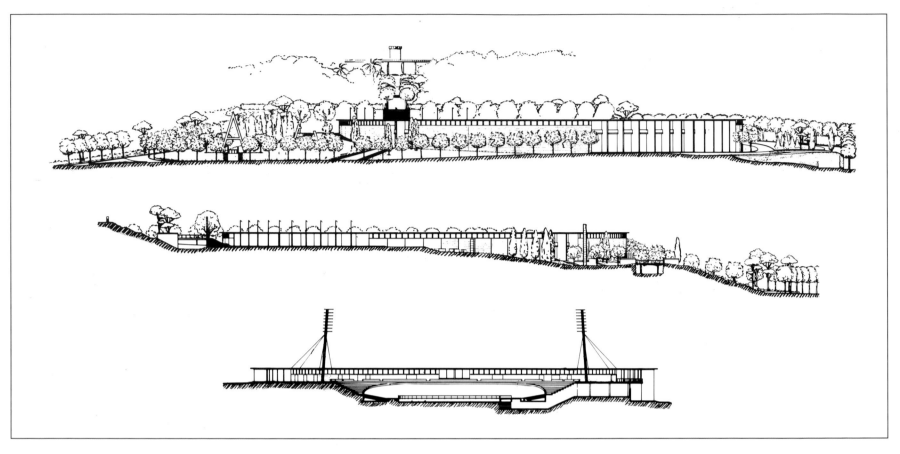

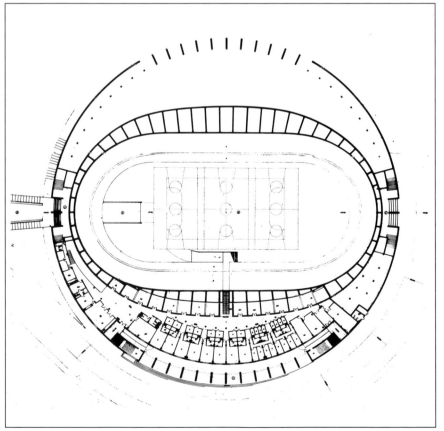

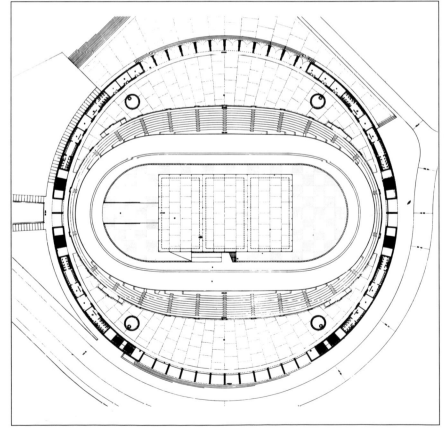

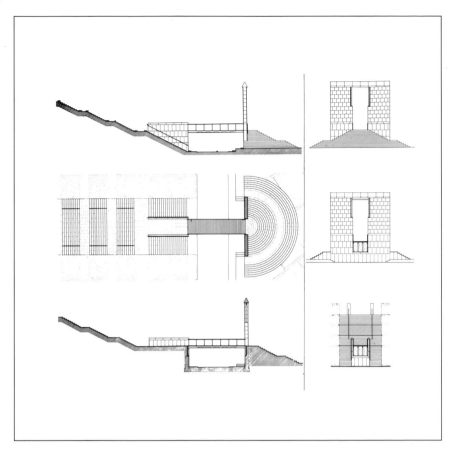

Architects: Jaume Bach/Gabriel Mora

Assistants: Josep Crivillers, Carles Oliver

Sports installations: Gerardo García-Ventosa, architect

Structures: Robert Brufau, architect

# Gràcia sports complex

## Gràcia, Barcelona    1986-1989

Gràcia is one of the most densely populated districts of Barcelona, to the extent that it might be said that its only open spaces are its public squares. As in many other neighborhoods of the central part of the city and the historic centre, there is a lack of amenities, in particular sports facilities.

There were two alternatives available for siting the sports center: either underground, beneath the Plaça del Diamant, or on a relatively spacious gap site. The first alternative would have been both costly and highly complicated, so the second option was chosen: to build above ground, on a plot in carrer Perill measuring 112 × 97 feet.

The project is best approached through the section. A ground floor for access leads down to a basement level with changing rooms, with the double-height squash courts at the end, connecting back visually with the vestibule.

The first floor, which contains the changing rooms for the swimming pool and the tank of the pool itself, is level with the +6.5 m mark of the surface of the block's interior courtyard.

The second floor contains the areas most used by the public, on the same level as the new open space provided by the recovery of the interior courtyard for public use. This floor houses the gym, the 20 m swimming pool, which receives sunlight through the glazed solarium, and the restaurant-bar, part of the plot which articulates the more private space of the swimming pool and the outdoor multi-sports court. This second floor is connected directly with the vestibule by way of a great staircase, which is the formally dominant element of the scheme.

Finally, the third floor is occupied by the multi-sports court, roofed with a lightweight metal structure.

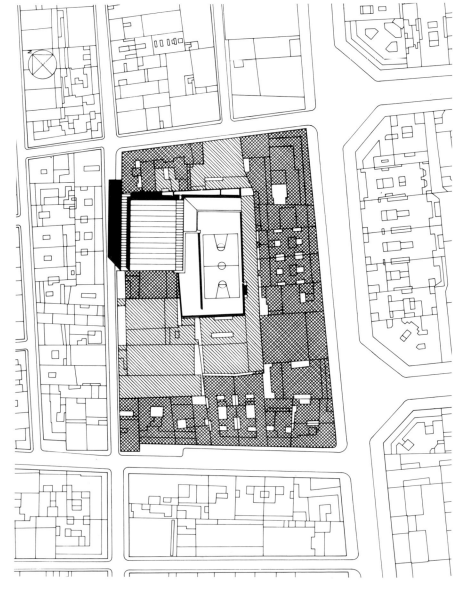

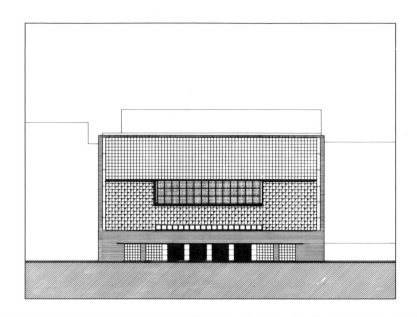

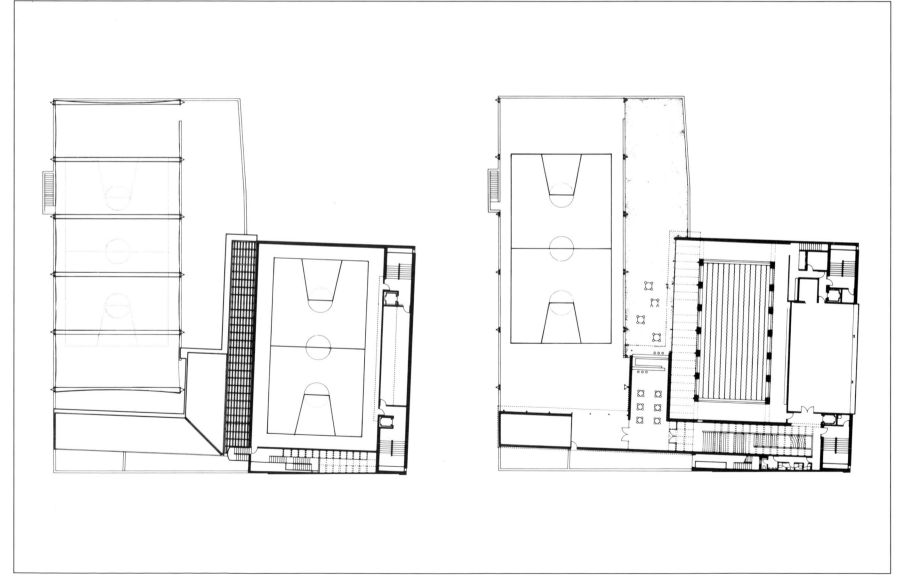

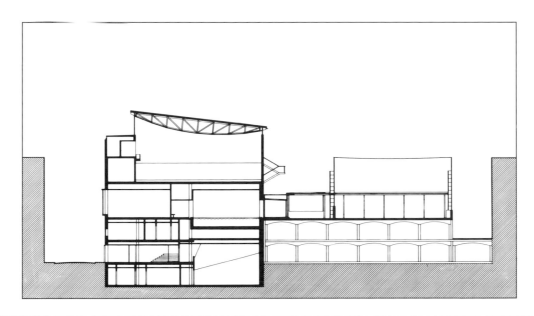

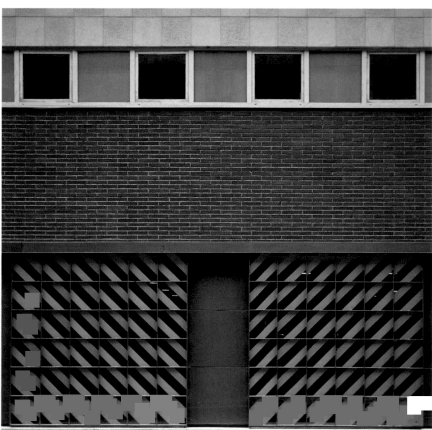

# Cultural facilities

Renovation of the central nucleus of the Archaeological Museum

Art Museum of Catalonia

Barcelona Pavilion

Santa Mònica Arts Centre

Museum of Contemporary Art

Tàpies Foundation

National Theater of Catalonia

Renovation and extension of the Gran Teatre del Liceu

Remodelling of the Palau de la Música Catalana

Architect: Josep Llinàs

Assistants: Jaume Martí, Josep Vicens Martí,
Jaume Camps

Structures: Robert Brufau, architect

# Renovation of the central nucleus of the Archaeological Museum

**Montjuïc, Barcelona    1986-1989**

This building, opened in 1929 as a Palace of the Graphic Arts and in 1932 converted to an Archaeological Museum, is extremely elementary in its organization. The plan is ordered around a hexagonal volume, from which the great galleries radiate out.

A series of small-scale renovations of the museum had combined to obscure the true scale of the building, which the refurbishment set out to recover.

This present scheme is at the same time the first stage of a long term project which will transform the first floor to the museum's public floor, with the services and main hall on the ground floor. This first phase consists in remodelling the central nucleus as the new main hall and providing access routes to the first floor.

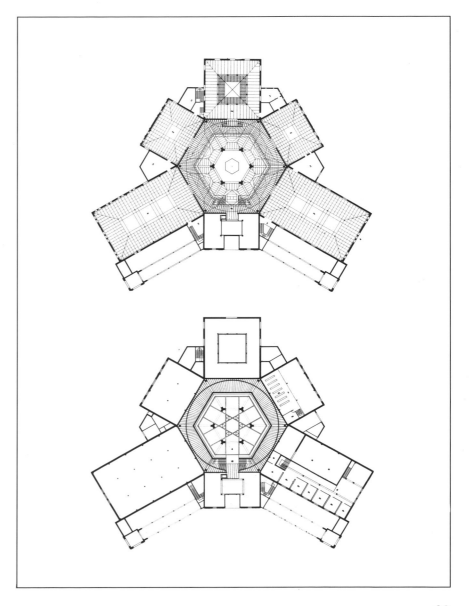

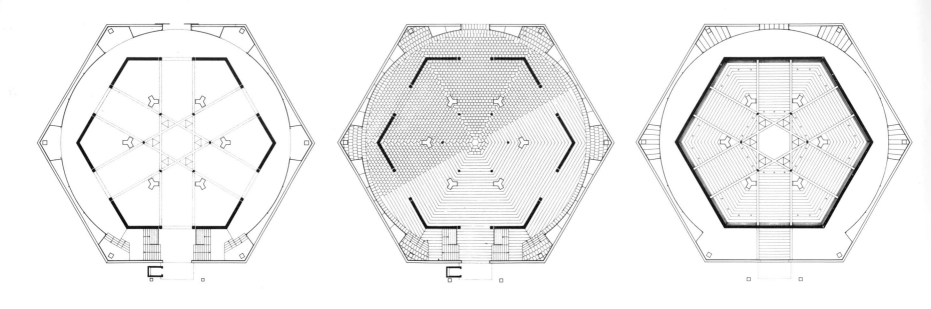

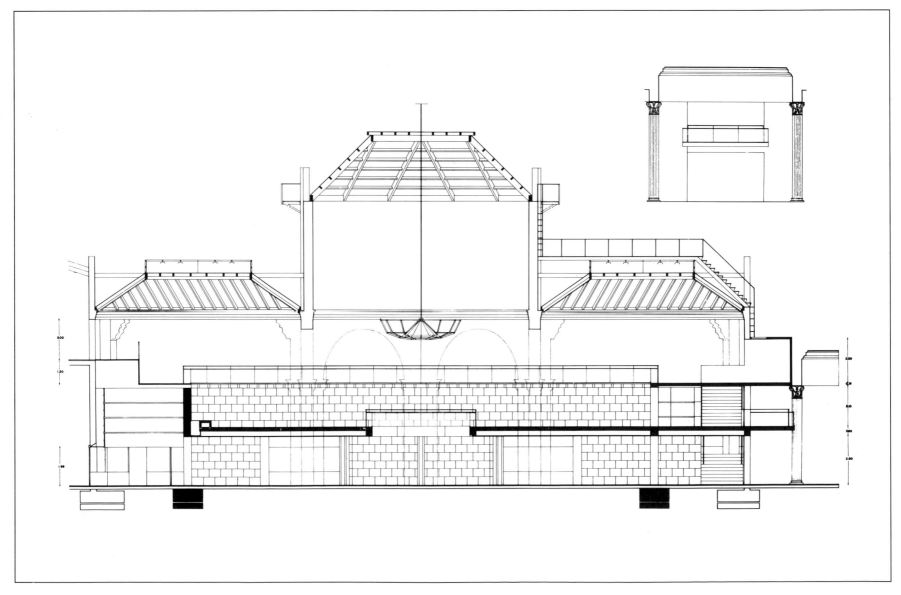

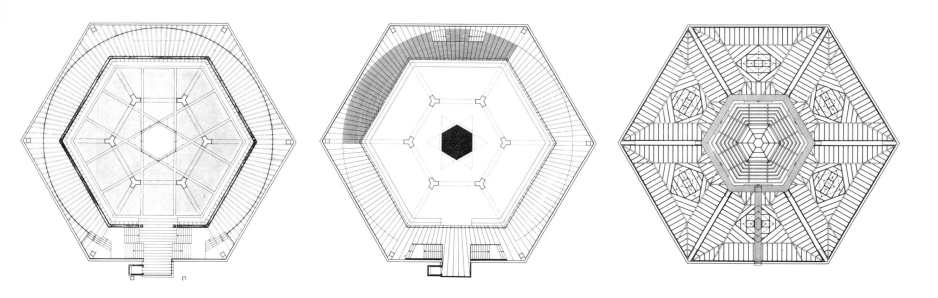

101

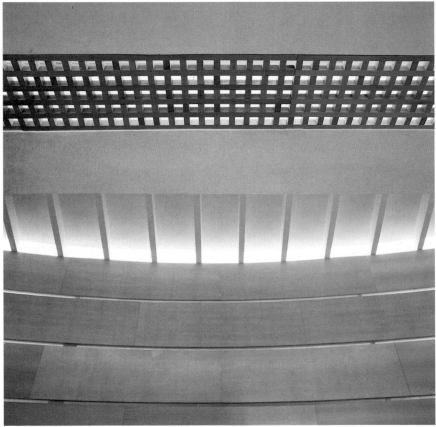

Architects: Gae Aulenti/Enric Steegmann

Assistants: Valerie Bergeron, Monique Bonadei,
Emil Palou, José Manuel Quiñoa, Giuseppe Raboni,
Josep Maria Serra, Piero Castiglioni, Joan Gallostra,
Angel Sánchez

Structures: Joan Ovejero

# Art Museum of Catalonia

## Montjuïc, Barcelona    1985-1992

The ceremonial Palau Nacional, originally designed by Pere Domènech as the grand museum of the 1929 International Exhibition, is a building with a curious typological and stylistic mix. This circumstance, together with the nature of the Art Museum of Catalonia's collections, was studied on the basis of an analytical method, which served to bring about the changes in perception necessary for a new type of exhibition space.

Vertical courtyards have been opened up, and, for reasons related to the structural independence of the grand hall and the cupola, the entire stair apparatus leading up to the first floor has been completely redesigned, bringing natural light into the main vestibule.

Two horizontal courtyards have been created on the first floor, providing views of the exterior from inside the building. This solution offers visitors the opportunity to relate the interior to the exterior, allowing them to be conscious of their position and orientation.

The grand hall has been conceived as a dynamic part of any visit to the museum, but it has also been treated as an autonomous element, in order for it to represent, in functional terms, the characteristic identity of the museum.

The library, on the other hand, is fitted inside the great dome in such a way that its identity extends out to the lateral courtyards which are, in turn, the identifying element as regards the museum and the building as a whole.

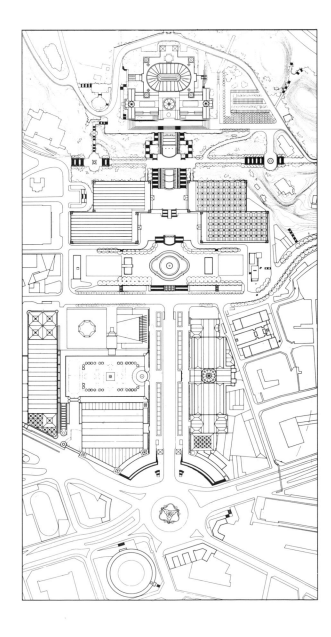

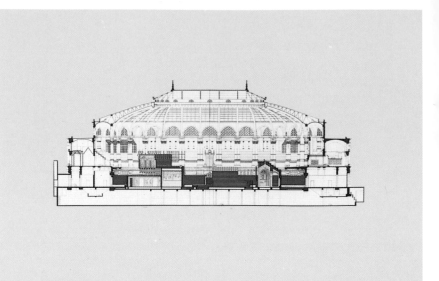

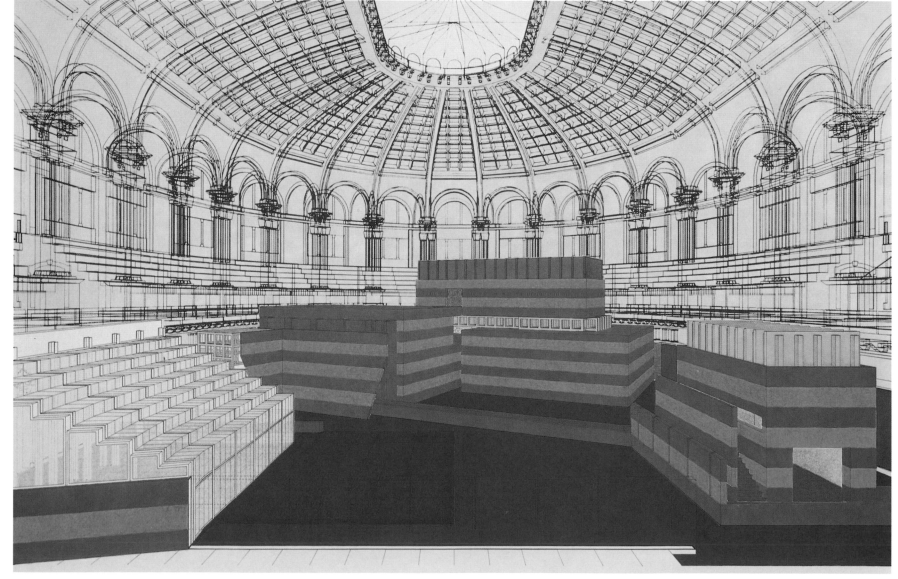

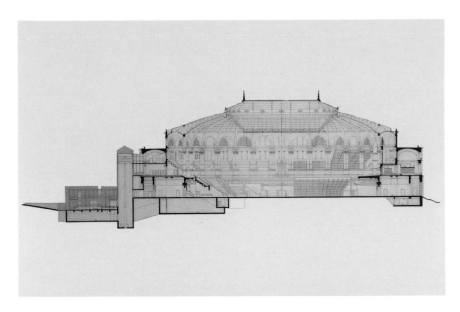

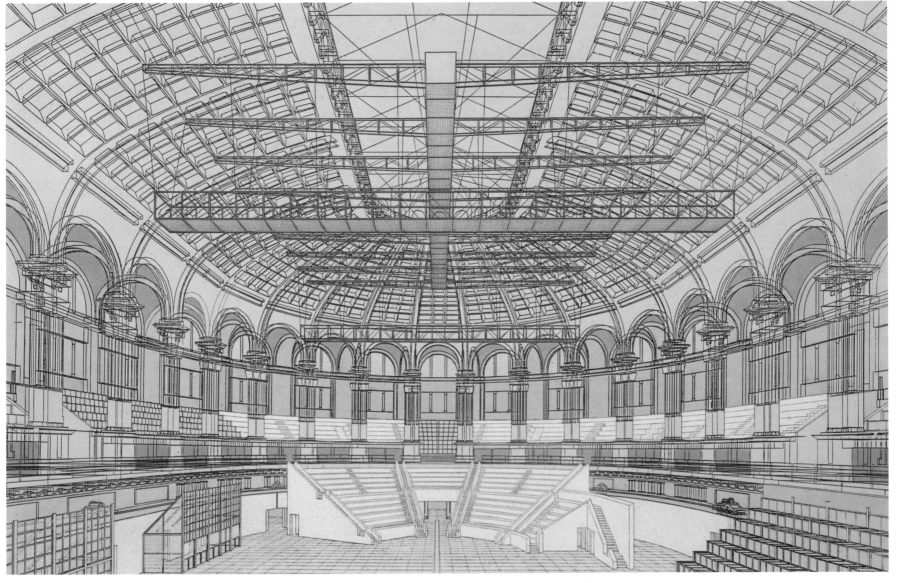

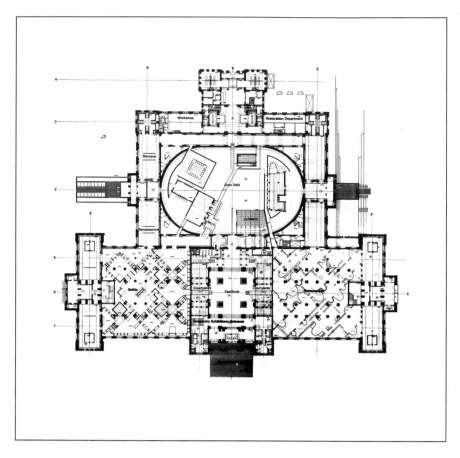

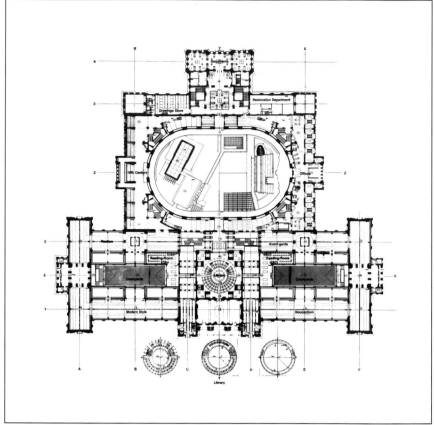

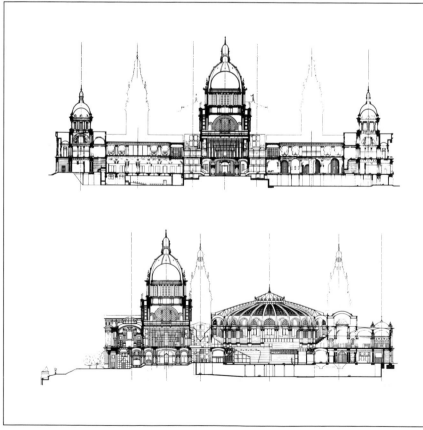

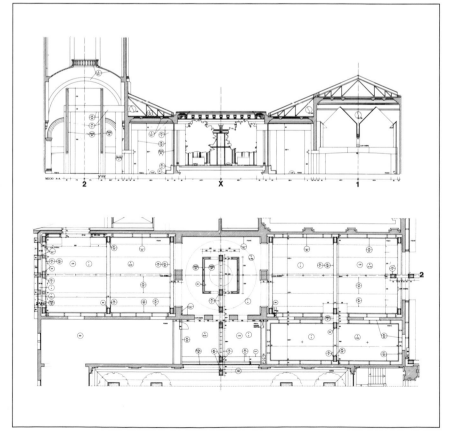

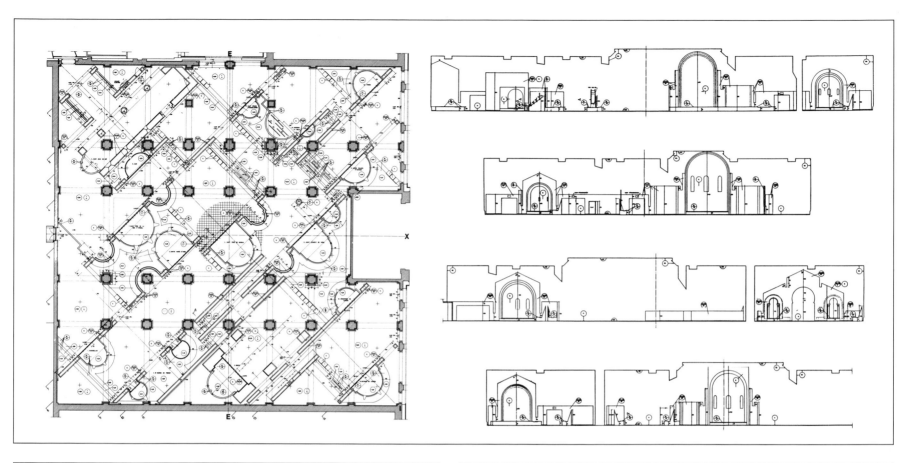

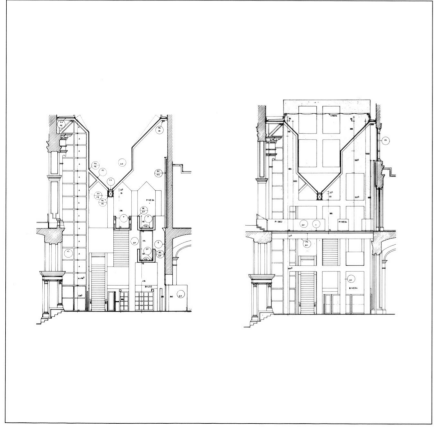

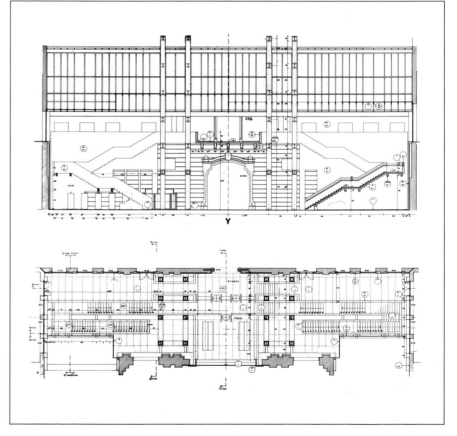

Architect: Ludwig Mies van der Rohe

Architects in charge of reconstruction: Cristian Cirici/
Fernando Ramos/Ignasi de Solà-Morales

Sculpture: Georg Kolbe

# Barcelona Pavilion

## Montjuïc, Barcelona 1929; 1984-1986

The Barcelona Pavilion has been acclaimed by critics and architects as one of the milestones of modern architecture. It is, in effect, one of the few manifestations of the contemporary spirit which justifies comparison with the great architects of the past, and it is to be regretted that it only existed during the International Exhibition of 1929.

These words of Philip C. Johnson's open the description of Mies van der Rohe's Barcelona Pavilion in the catalogue for the exhibition New York's Museum of Modern Art devoted to him in 1947. Between that and the Mies centenary exhibition of 1986, also organized by MOMA, a Barcelonese initiative, first put forward in 1954 and supported by Mies himself, bore fruit in the form of the pristine reconstruction of the Pavilion, fifty-seven years after its inauguration.

The reconstruction of a building of such capital importance for twentieth century architecture is a profoundly risky undertaking. Particularly so when the piece of work has never ceased to constitute an obligatory point of reference for coalescing ideas and aims of avant-garde European architecture in this century.

While the building of a replica might seem to be a trivial operation, it must be confessed that its completion gave those involved great satisfaction. In the same way as a knowledge of the work of a great musician of the past asks to be completed by playing it, it may be that in this case the genuine quality of the design by Mies van der Rohe asks to be contemplated in its true dimensions and the direct physical perception of its colors.

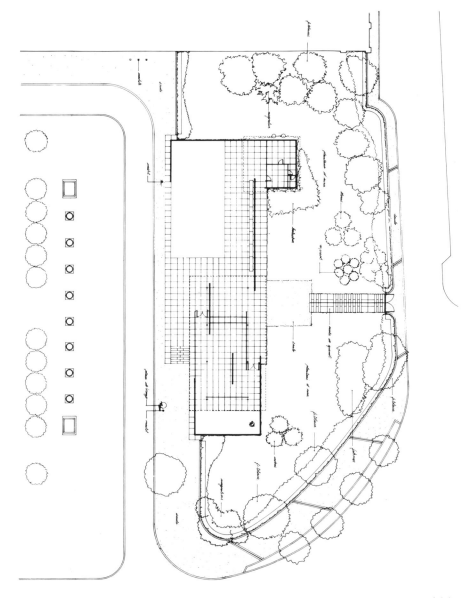

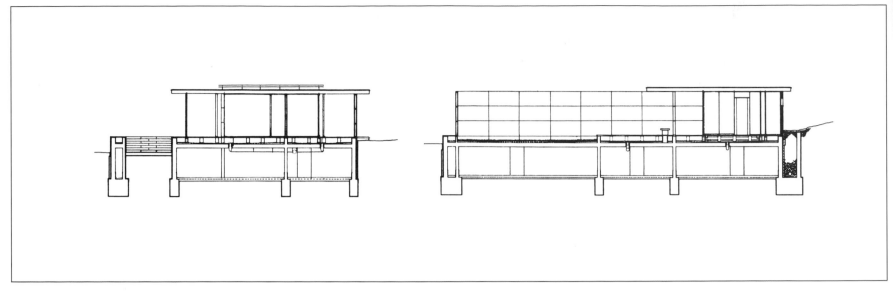

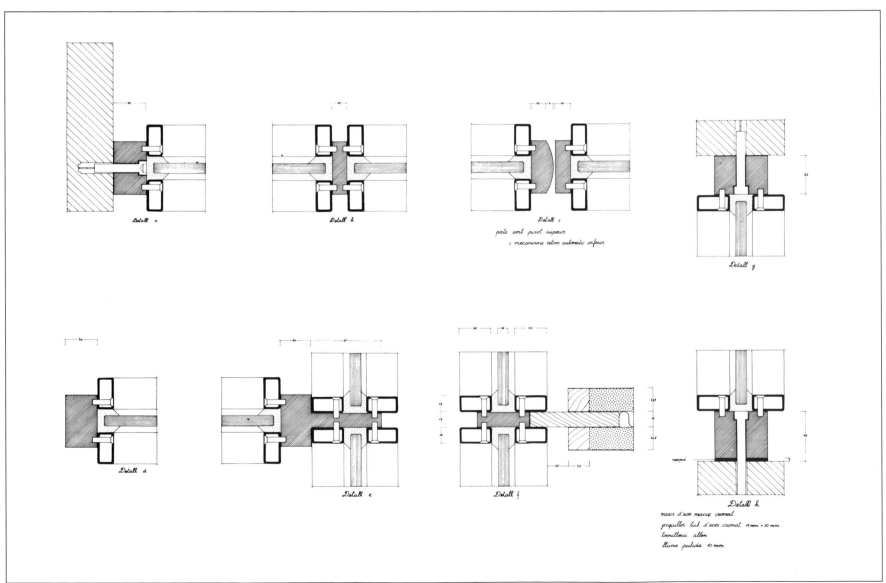

Detall a

Detall b

Detall c
porta amb pivot superior
i mecanisme retorn automàtic inferior

Detall g

Detall d

Detall e

Detall f

Detall h

marcs d'acer massís cromat
perquilles tub d'acer cromat 15 mm x 30 mm
cargolería allen
lluna pulida 10 mm

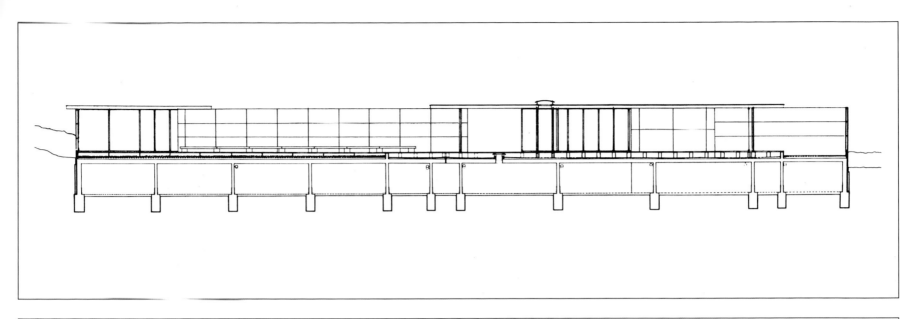

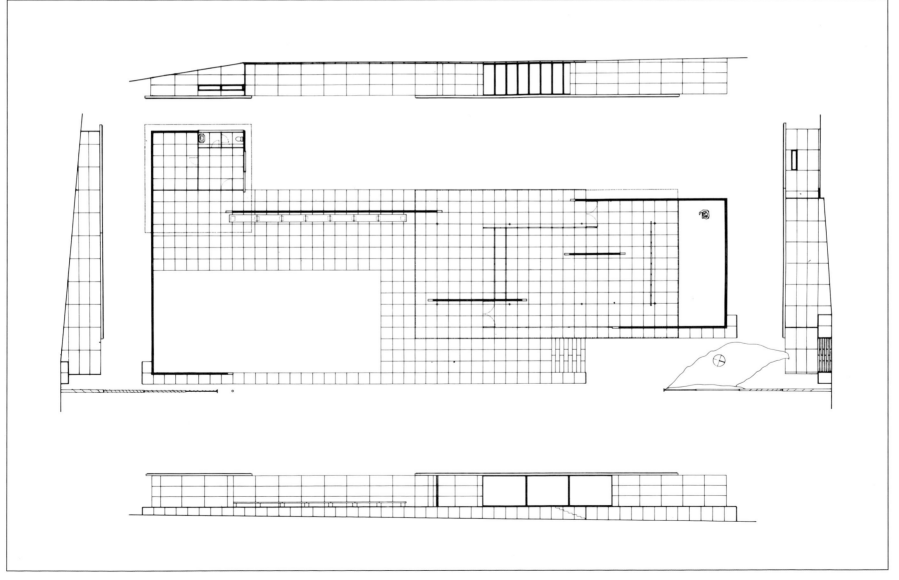

Architects: Albert Viaplana/Helio Piñón
Assistant: Ricard Mercadé

# Santa Mónica Arts Centre

**Barcelona    1985-1989**

In the words of the architects:

"There is less to say every time.

Somebody built a temple inside the old Convent of Santa Mónica; we built a platform at the entrance.

Later we stretched out a veil inside the temple for those who came after to show their work under.

We found, too, that somebody else had demolished the later volume which completed the whole; to commemorate it, we brought the void outside.

In the facade we see the convex, the transparent, the ligneous, the light, the rectilinear, the concave, the opaque, the lithic, the heavy, the curving; each one in its place.

The grin of the Cheshire cat, under a cornice, slowly disappears."

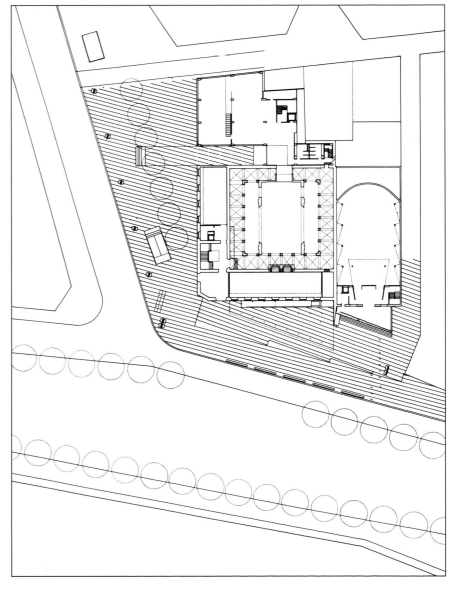

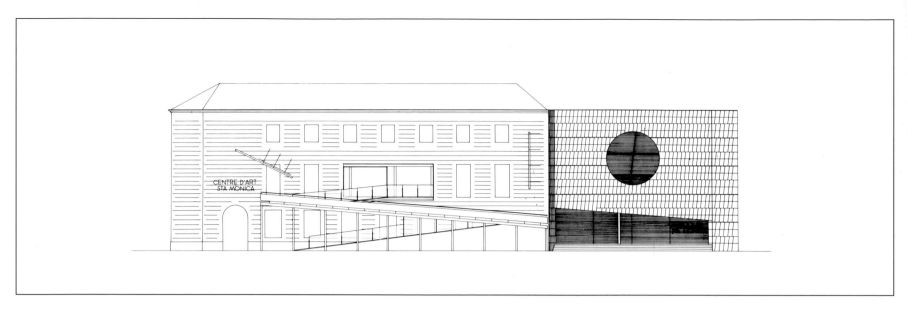

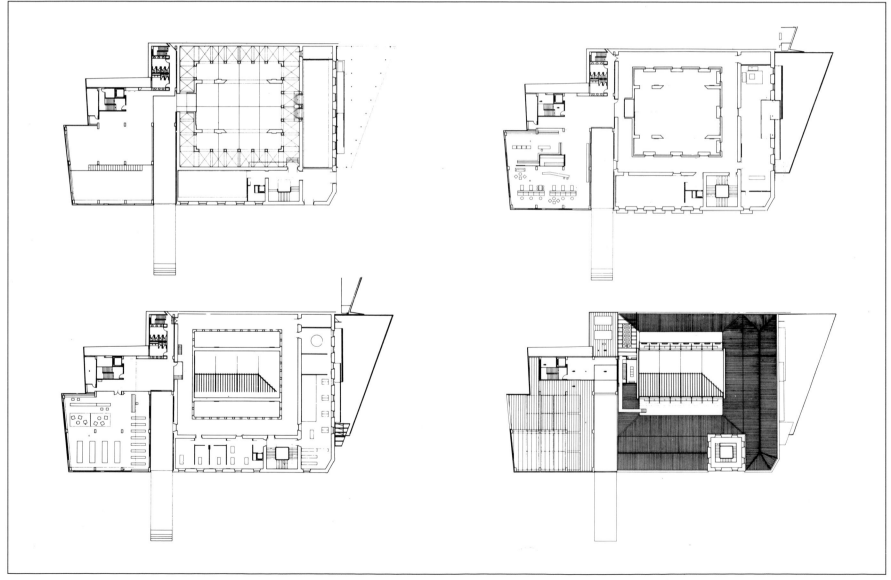

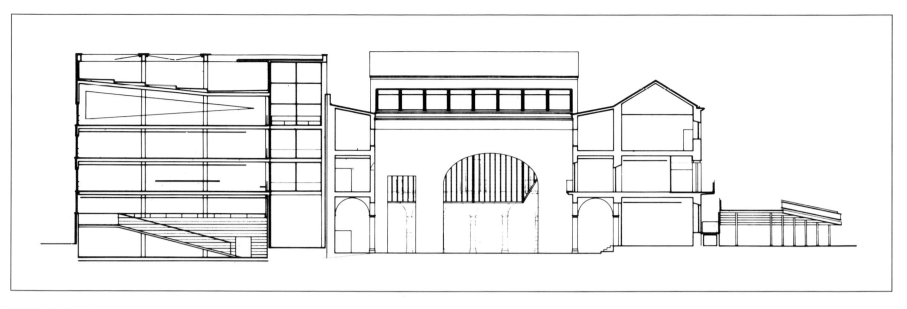

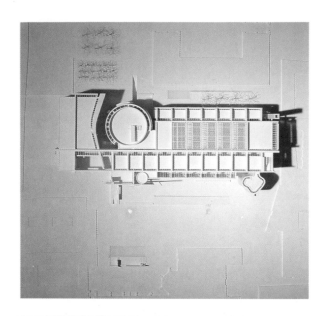

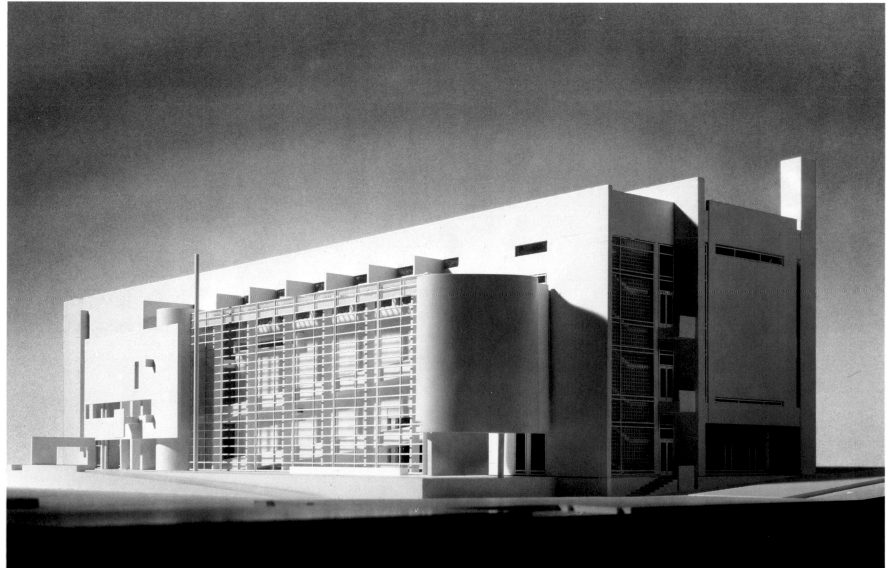

Architects: Richard Meier & Partners

Design Team: Richard Meier, Thomas Phifer

Collaborators: Renny Logan, Project Architect; Daniel Brown,
Steve Dayton, Debbie Lieber,
Jonathan Marvel, Gilbert Rampy, David Schilling,
Madeleine Sánchez

Associate architects: F. J. Ramos i Associats – TDR

# Museum of Contemporary Art

## Barcelona    1987-1992

Situated in the area of the Casa de la Caritat, formerly used as a
hospice, the Barcelona Museum of Contemporary Art sets up a
dialogue between the historical forms of its context and its function as
centre for the exhibition of contemporary art.

The building is reached by means of an exterior ramp which connects
with the ground floor. Circulation continues by way of an interior ramp,
situated inside the great triple-height vestibule, up to the two floors
above. The large vestibule, in addition to its role as a point of reference
and distribution, acts as a filter for the natural light needed by the
interior exhibition spaces.

Various different types of exhibition space are envisaged: from loft-type
open plan areas, intended to accomodate large temporary exhibitions,
to more intimate spaces suited to the contemplation of smaller-scale
works of art.

The museum program also includes an education service, a
specialized library, a shop and a café adjacent to the sculpture garden.

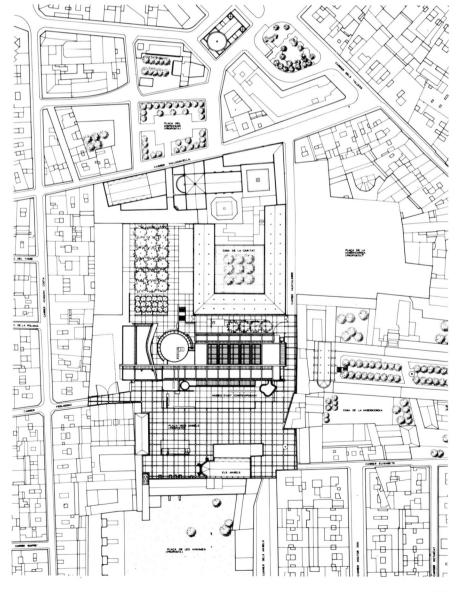

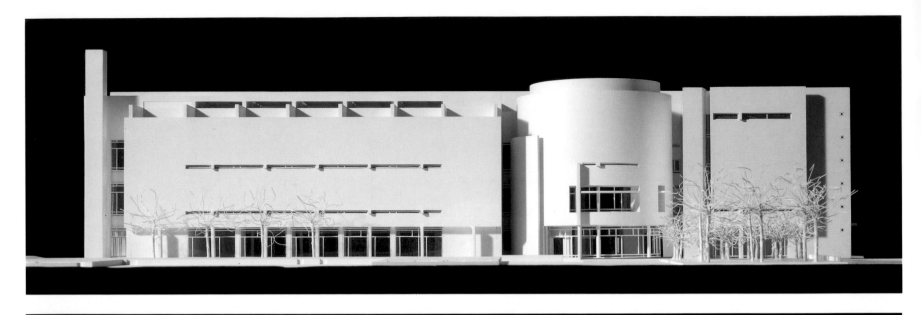

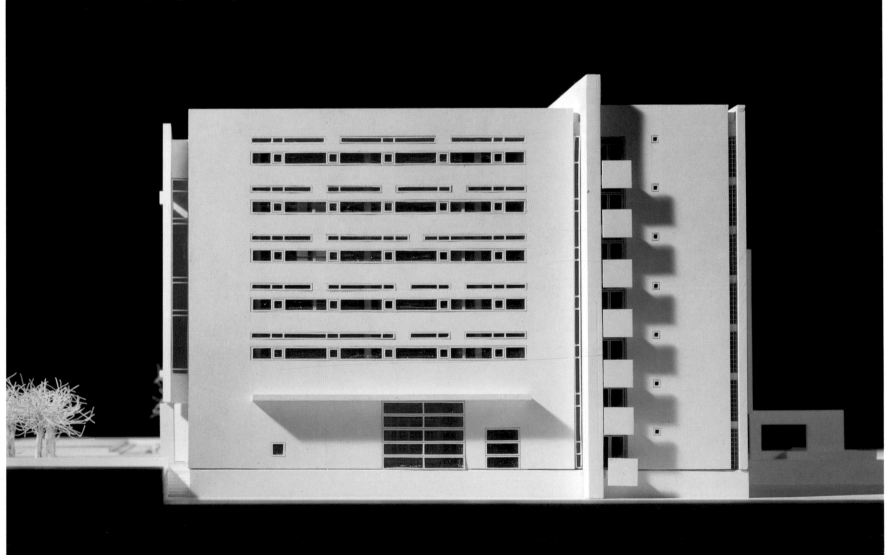

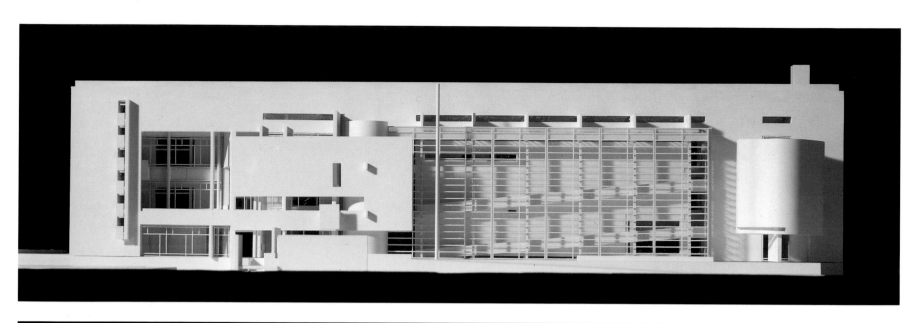

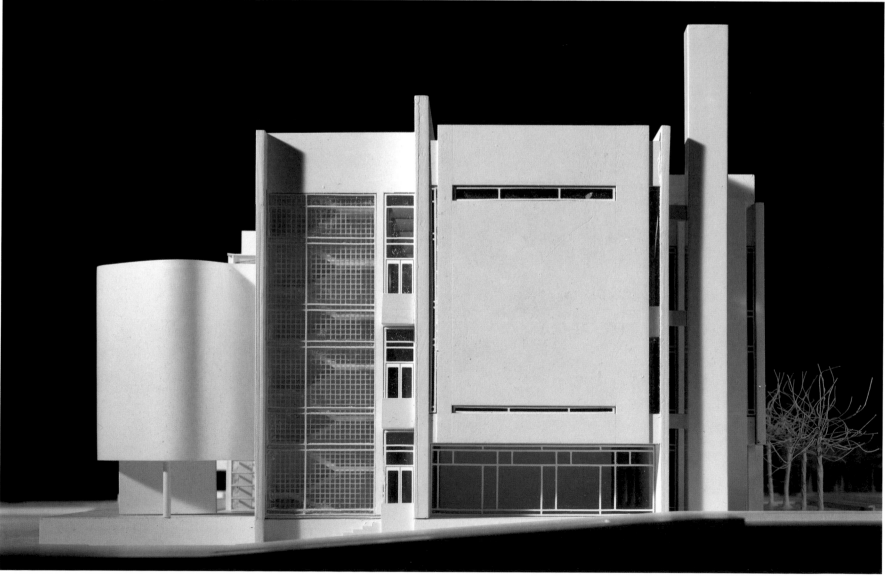

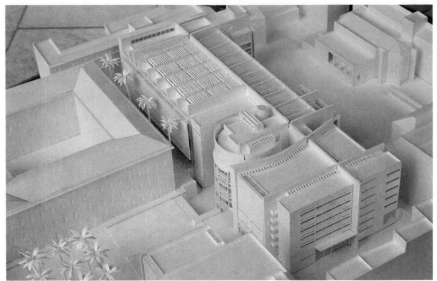

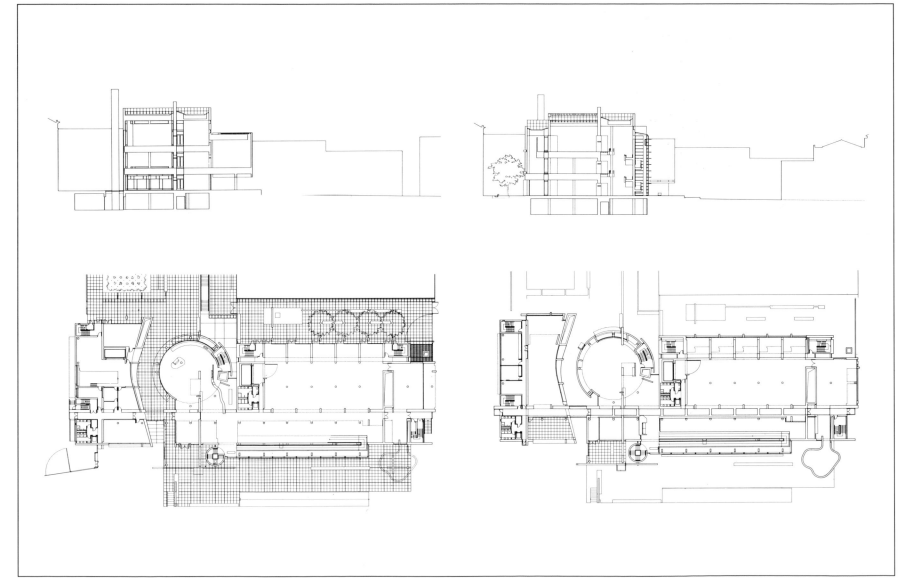

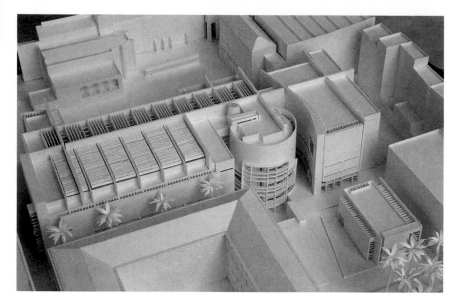
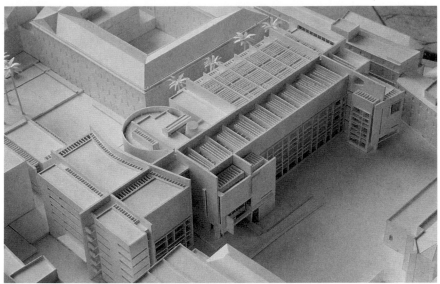
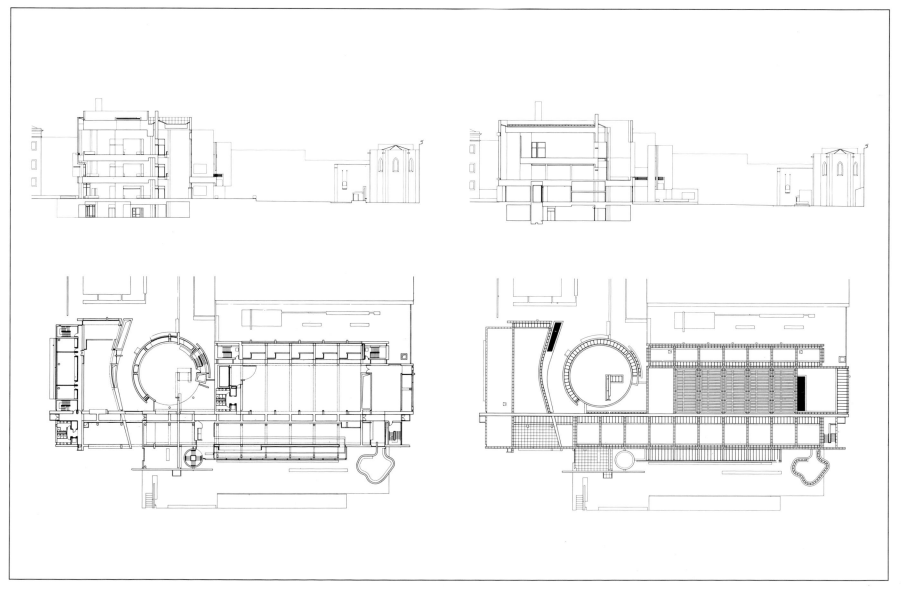

Architects: Roser Amadó/Lluís Domènech

Assistants: Ramon Domènech, Anton Alsina, Joan Gallostra

Structures: Agustí Obiols, architect

Sculpture: Antoni Tàpies

# Tàpies Foundation

**Barcelona    1986-1990**

This centre for contemporary art, which houses a significant part of the work of the Catalan painter Antoni Tàpies, is located in the former offices of the publishing house Montaner y Simón, by the *Modernista* architect Lluís Domènech i Montaner. The building dates from 1879, and ranks as an early milestone in Catalan *Modernisme.*

The project sets out from the idea of recovering the original technological, spatial and aesthetic values of the existing building, with its large spaces and overhead light, adapting these to its new function. To this end, the scheme seeks to interpret the building's spatial characteristics, understanding this as a horizontal sequence of three spaces: a main volume giving onto the street, an interior volume of large rooms, and a lower part to the rear within the central courtyard of the city block. The sloping form of the roof corresponds to the classical *impluvium.*

Basically, the new intervention is centred on the design and introduction of new staircases which connect the various parts of the institution. The exhibition areas are located in the space formerly occupied by the publishers' offices. At the rear of the ground floor is an all-purpose hall, in the volume of the present-day courtyard. The upper level accomodates the ticket desk and bookshop. The space beneath this is occupied by the storeroom and the print room. The first floor has been conceived as the site for more exclusive activities such as the library and general archives, reading and conference room, and a salon for temporary exhibitions. The second floor houses the administration offices. There is sufficient space in the basement for a storeroom and another exhibition room. Continuing the existing structure of the skylights on the roof and following the order of the building's structure, eight projecting beams support an arrangement of transparent metal grids which in turn serves as the support for a sculptural work by Antoni Tàpies, drawing attention to the building's new identity as an art gallery.

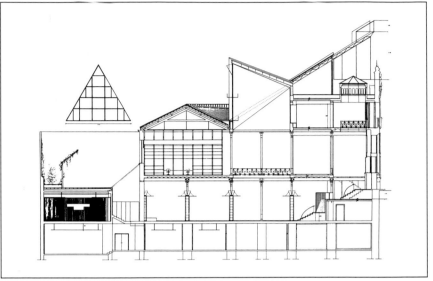

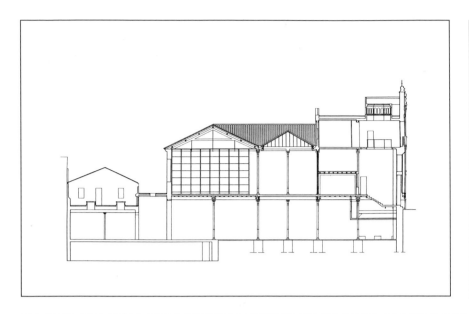

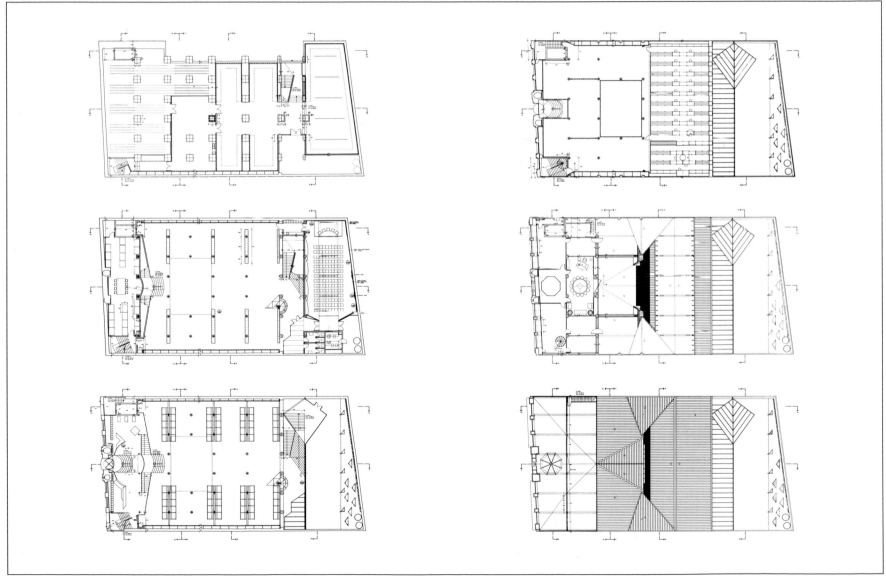

132

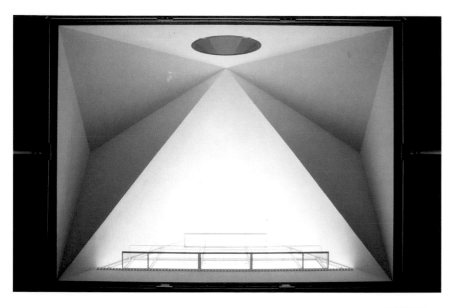

Architect: Ricardo Bofill – Taller de Arquitectura

Associate architect: Jean-Pierre Carniaux

Assistants: X. Grau, E. Wachs, S. Strum, D. Baker

Structures: F. Rubio

# National Theater of Catalonia

## Barcelona    1989-1992

The National Theater of Catalonia is a theater complex composed of two separate buildings which, together with the auditorium designed by Rafael Moneo, will make up the largest cultural center in Barcelona.

The complex is situated alongside the Plaça de les Glòries, the remodelling of which is currently under investigation, to conform with the need to locate major cultural amenities on the outskirts of the city injecting new life into these areas. The study draws attention to the importance of this sector of Barcelona, the junction of the city's main axes (Gran Via, Meridiana and Diagonal), and illustrates the opportunity of connecting the edge of the Eixample with the Olympic Village, extending the Ciutadella Park with a pedestrian walkway, and bringing about the transformation of this part of Barcelona into a veritable gateway to the city.

The National Theater of Catalonia has been conceived as a monumental landmark for the city; this explains the simplicity of its volume. The building, of great technical efficiency, has a double skin: an outer layer consisting of a "Planar" curtain wall, and an inner layer of architectural concrete. The aim was to bring together the clear, simple volumes of the foyer, the auditorium and the stage under a single pitched roof of treated aluminium, resting on a framework of great three-dimensional triangular beams supported by pillars of architectural concrete.

The theater, with capacity for fifteen hundred spectators, is divided conceptually into three zones: the foyer, the auditorium and the "house".
– The foyer, anteroom to the performance, is glazed and full of plants. Brightly lit areas alternate with areas of shade, as in a greenhouse, an indoor garden where people can meet and interact.
– The auditorium, heart of the building, is circular in form, with a steep incline and no boxes, so that the audience is close to the stage, concentrated on the performance.
– A large house of glass, 39 feet high, envelops the foyer and the semicircular facade of the great auditorium, reminiscent of a Greek theater. Beneath the foyer is the experimental theater, with seats for four hundred spectators.

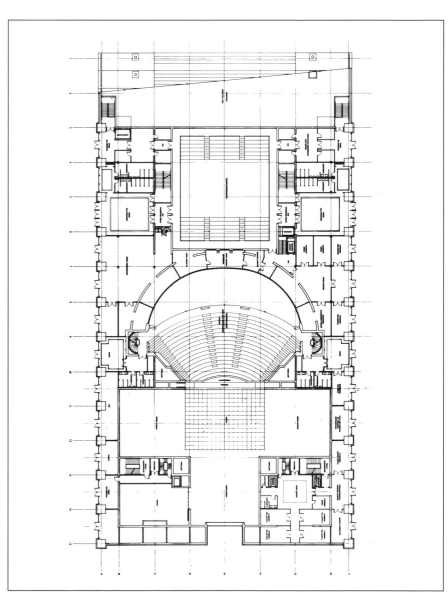

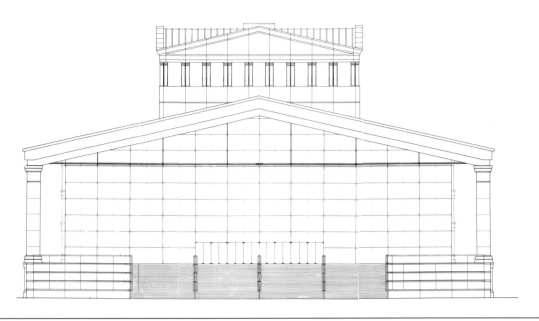

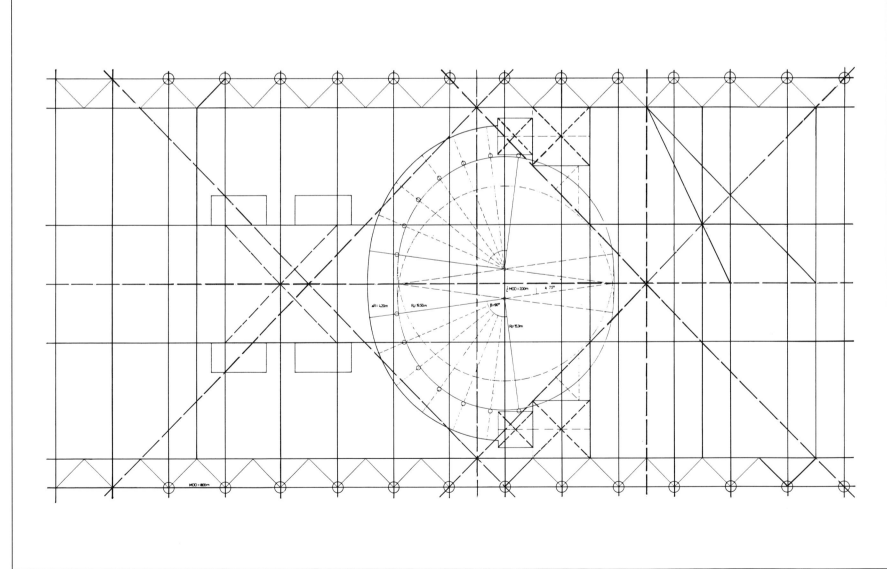

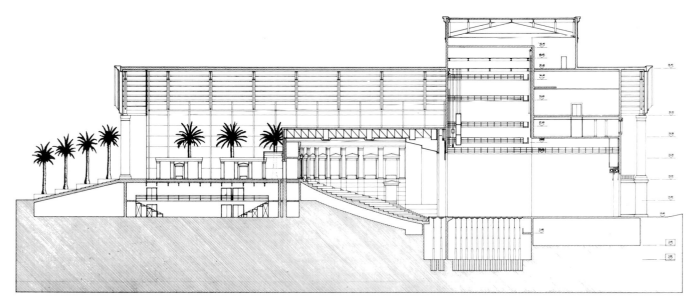

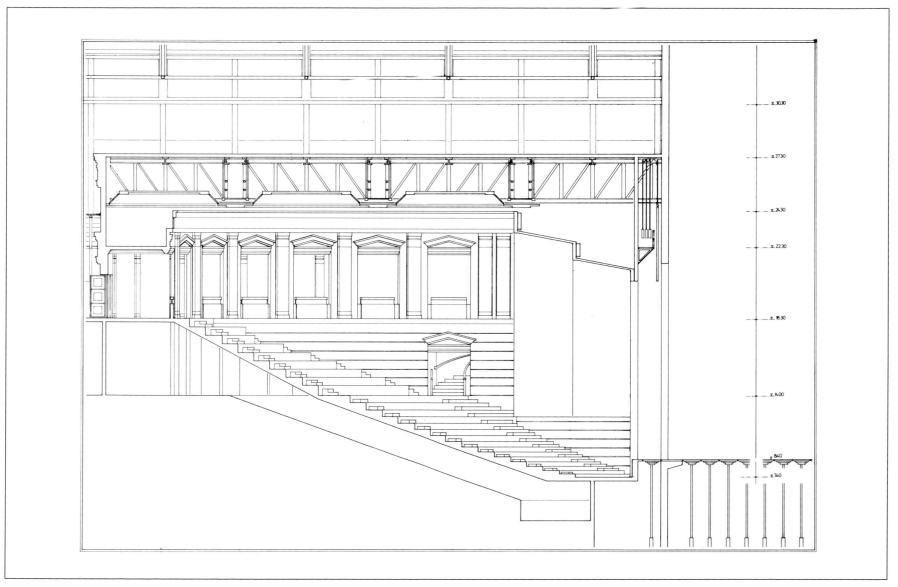

GRAN TEATRE DEL LICEU

Architect: Ignasi de Solà-Morales

Assistants: Xavier Fabré, Lluís Dilmé,
Jaume Benavent, architects

# Renovation and extension of the Gran Teatre del Liceu

## Barcelona 1987-

The initial study took as its point of departure a consideration of the deficiencies of the existing building. The modernization of the present facility envisages a major extension of available space to be achieved by taking over sites bordering the theater.

The conservation of the building's monumental elements is also a priority. The scheme proposes to conserve the Rambla facade and restore the Sant Pau facade. The new facades will follow the fundamental lines of composition of the existing building, utilizing a language expressive of its contemporary character.

With regard to the stage, the criteria adopted is the creation of a triple performance space.

Ease of access from the street is fundamental, as is the layout of the services related to the stage. The remodelling of various spaces is envisaged in order to create two new vertical distribution axes. The area bounding the new stage and the void of the auditorium will accomodate two blocks of offices.

The renovation will conclude with the adaptation of the central part of the basement and foyer as cloakrooms, services and a restaurant and bar.

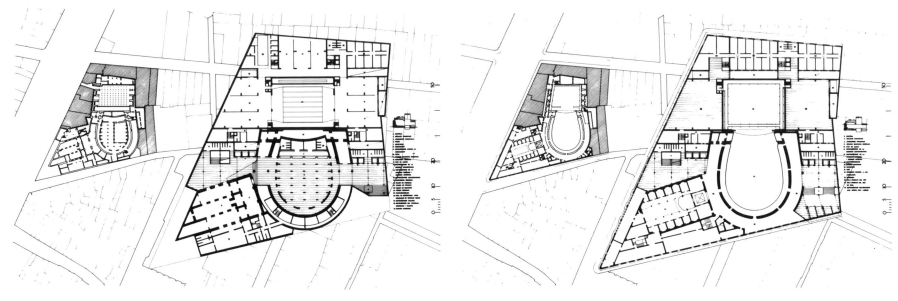

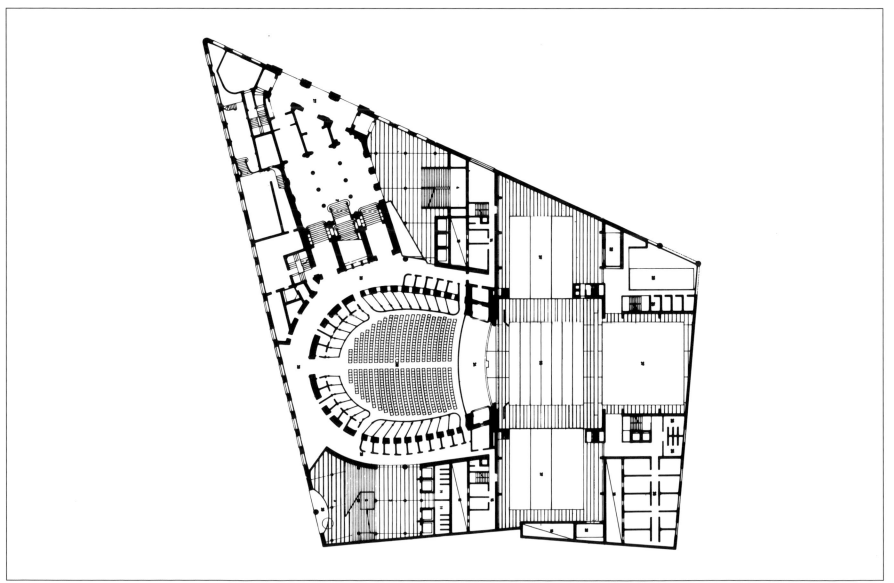

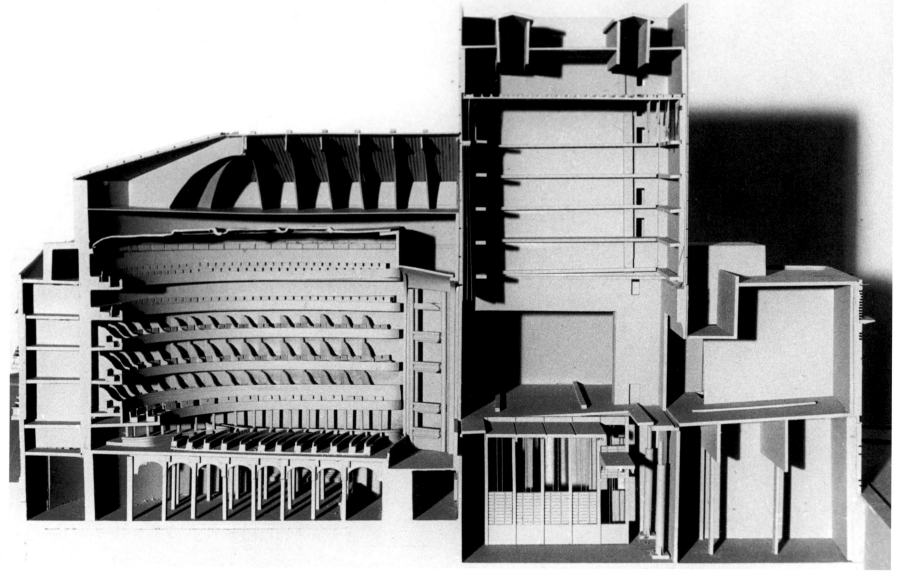

143

Architects: Tusquets, Díaz & Asociados
Oscar Tusquets and Carlos Díaz

Assistants: Matilde Correa, Claudia Mann, Josep Zazurca

Structures: Francesc Bassó, architect

# Remodelling of the Palau de la Música Catalana

## Barcelona   1982-1989

The fundamental idea of the project consisted in reducing the length of the Sant Francesc de Paula church, designed by E. P. Cendoya in 1940, and redefining the consequently vacant space.

To this end, a new apse was proposed where the transept was originally envisaged, so that while conserving a part of the church possessed of some dignity, the volume and cost of the building, which seemed to exceed the present needs of the parish, was reduced.

The space thus created has been used for the sacristy and other parish services, a small square which leads, surprisingly, to the Palau, and a new annex to the Palau.

The new construction calmly resolves all the deficiencies in the services of the existing building, and made it possible to free the Palau of the successive modifications which had gradually covered over Domènech's original work.

From the urban design point of view, the new building screens off the courtyard on the interior of the block. In addition, it offers a visual backdrop to carrer Ramon Mas, consisting of a tower centrally positioned on its axis.

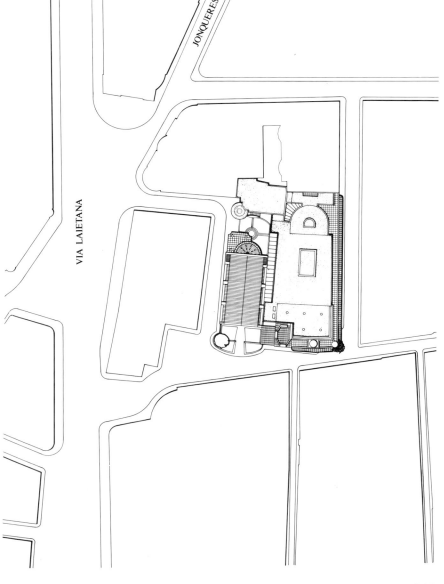

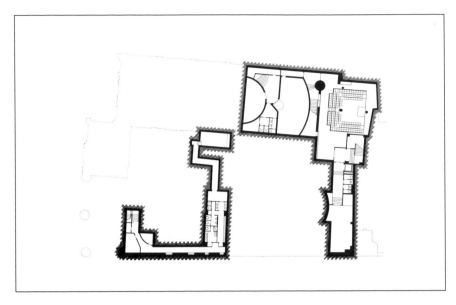

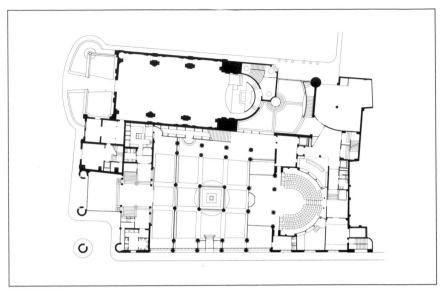

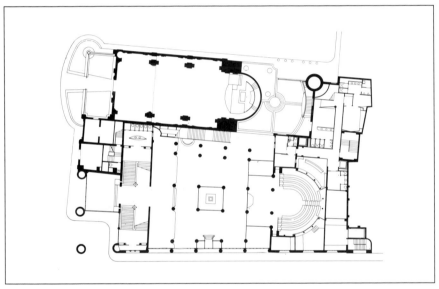

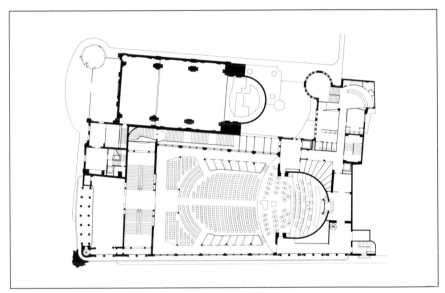

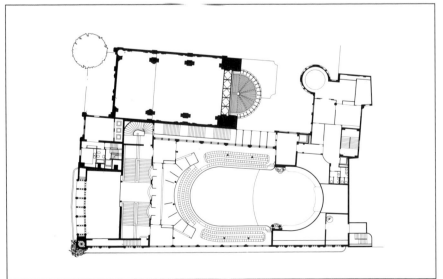

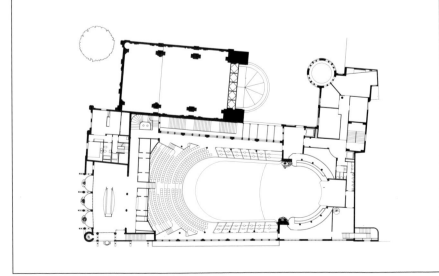

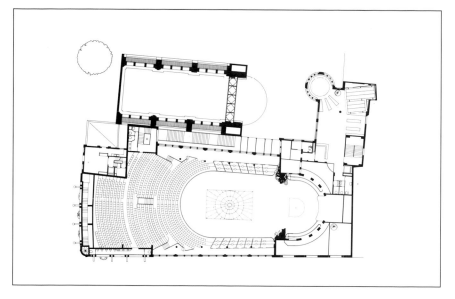

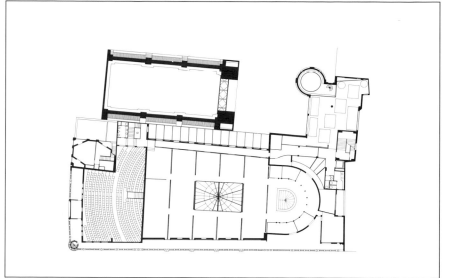

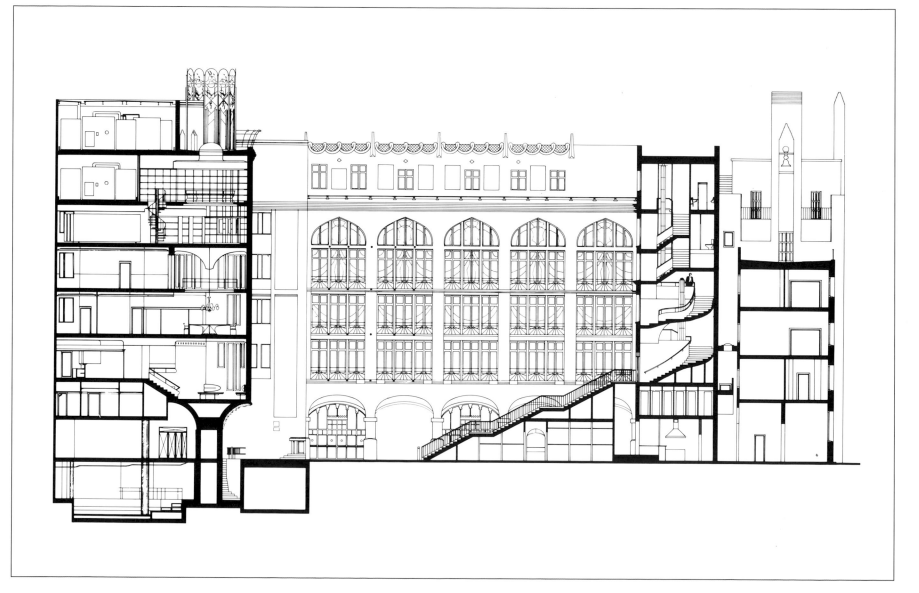

149

# Public spaces

Fossar de la Pedrera

Moll de la Fusta

Besòs Park in Sant Adrià de Besòs

Plaça dels Països Catalans

Bac de Roda-Felip II bridge

Plaça de la Palmera

Creueta del Coll park

Architect: Beth Galí

# Fossar de la Pedrera

## Barcelona   1983-1986

From the end of one the old roads running through the terraced cementery on Montjuïc, with its back to the sea, we arrive at a great excavation in the mountainside left by a disused quarry.

This quarry has served, historically, as a common grave, in which lie the bodies of many of those who gave their lives in defense of Catalan freedom.

The remodelling of this spot, abandoned now for many years, gives it dignity, and offers the fallen the remembrance. recognition and homage they deserve.

The concealed workings are reached by way of a road which twists around its own axis, only gradually arriving at the opening of the excavation, and denying the visitor a clear frontal view of the quarry. Having reached this point, a grove of cypresses and stone columns – engraved with the names of those who died in front of the firing squad in 1939 – acts as a filter, crowning the ascent to the central space. Here the tragic impact of the place makes itself fully apparent.

The minimal architectonic intervention seeks to capture and exalt the dramatic quality of the landscape. Great blocks of stone give solidity to the walls of the precinct, and an ample curve embraces the wide expanse of grass over the mass grave. The scheme at this point becomes more architectonic, drawing attention to particular elements of the composition.

The linear route, sheltered by the two-level fragile pergola, offers dynamic views across the greenery contained within the great hollow, leading on to the culmination of the procession: the tomb of the murdered president Lluís Companys.

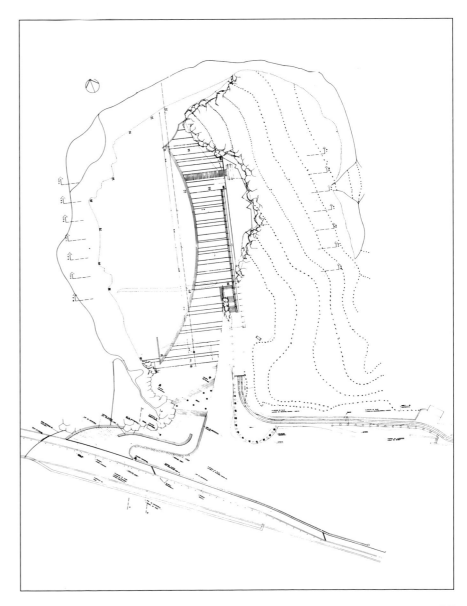

Architect: Manuel de Solà-Morales

Assistants: Oriol Clos, Joaquim Pascual, Josep Quintana, Jordi Torrella, Dolors Febles

Sculptures: Miquel Blay, Francisco López, Robert Krier, Robert Llimós

# Moll de la Fusta

## Barcelona   1981-1987

The execution of the project for the Moll de la Fusta involved a beginning attempt to remodel the city's waterfront at its most difficult stretch. The overall plan divides the passage of the Cinturó del Litoral ring road between the old city and the sea – a typical problem of seaports – into different sections. It also organizes spaces for car parking and a pedestrian area for strolling in, with small shops, cafés and restaurants. The plan proposes the partial suppression of one of the central quays, in order to give a new configuration to the expanse of water as a unified space on a larger scale, stretching from Montjuïc to the Barceloneta.

The project for the Moll de la Fusta is the first phase of this operation: the densest kilometer of urban seafront on the Mediterranean. The space is formally organized in three distinct units which are visually and functionally interrelated. The architectonic neutrality and expressive restraint of the means employed have resulted in a strong sense of the site as a metropolitan setting with the dynamic perception and forms which public use gives to the spaces. The aim was to create a complex yet single urban space, expressly endowing the design of the different elements with a minimal, anecdotal and conventional value whenever possible.

The spatial scale sought by the urban design project paves the way for subsequent design operations on a smaller scale, such as the interior decoration of the cafés, the sculptures by Llimós and Krier, or the advantageous use made of the existing streetlamps.

165

Architects: Albert Viaplana/Helio Piñón

# Besòs Park in Sant Adrià de Besòs

## Sant Adrià de Besòs, Barcelona    1982-1987

The architects state: "We designed a place, not a park. When originally posing the problem, all that we put into the project was the will to construct it. We had, therefore, to invent the place and, on this occasion, its creator. For a few brief moments we were giants, capable of levelling the terrain with one hand, before going on to trace out with the index finger of the other the corridors in which to situate the vegetation that will endow the place with meaning. We sheltered it to the north and opened it up to the sea. The spaces left between these wide strips of vegetation have been organized according to the disposition ordained by chance: a whimsical fountain over a slightly damp cup, a corner with a romantic bench, some concrete spheres and pyramids, scattered by some obscure order, some linear galleries, a monumental gate, a tree-lined avenue with a surprising course, and so on. Two Y-shaped walkways cross the site in accordance with their own exclusive law."

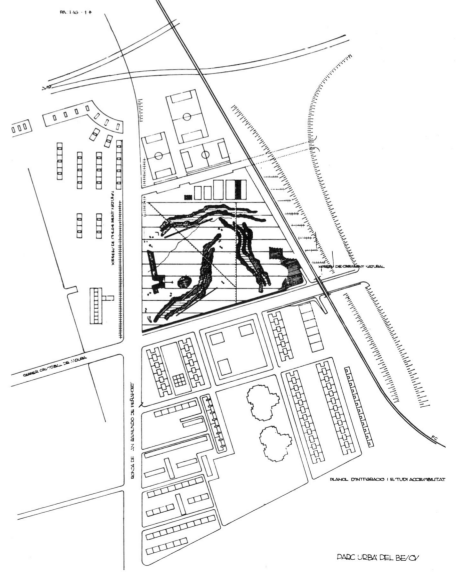

Architects: Albert Viaplana/Helio Piñón

Assistant: Enric Miralles, architect

# Plaça dels Països Catalans

## Sants, Barcelona    1981-1983

At the outset we were desolate. Anyone who knows the place we had to work on will understand. But we didn't complain too much; we didn't complain at all. We concluded that from that moment the project alone would have to contain the feelings the place inspired. Astuteness is indispensable in our profession, and silence is one of its forms. With a knowing smile we planned a horizontal surface so as to bring together all parts of the site, even the most intractable, in the manner of a road as broad as it was long. But even the existing streets were lost in that desert, and the walking figure was left with no alternative but to stay still. On the one hand, there was the urge to spread out in all directions, and find a balance that way, like water poured over the floor; but there was also the knowledge that stillness, like the silence before it, makes what was then far now near, what was then closed now open, and makes the inanimate start to move. Things situated themselves in front, behind, above, below, inside or out; the silence becomes as audible as a scream and noises fall to a murmur, because, for one instant, you are the center of everything. The water that was spilt dwindles to a little patch on the floor, and the floor curls like something left too long in the oven. The most remarkable thing was that the more we concentrated on each part of the project, the emptier the city became, and more space opened up for doubt, the unknown, the opposite of what was being asserted. In spite of everything, desolation was now bearable.

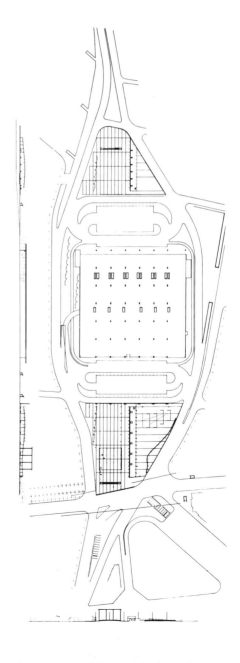

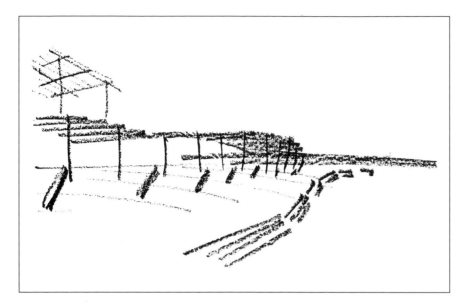

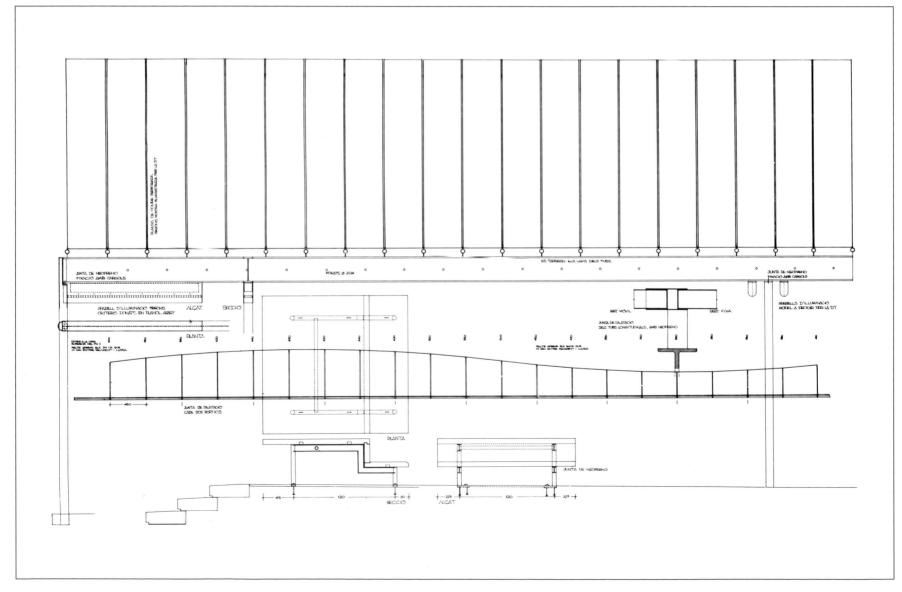

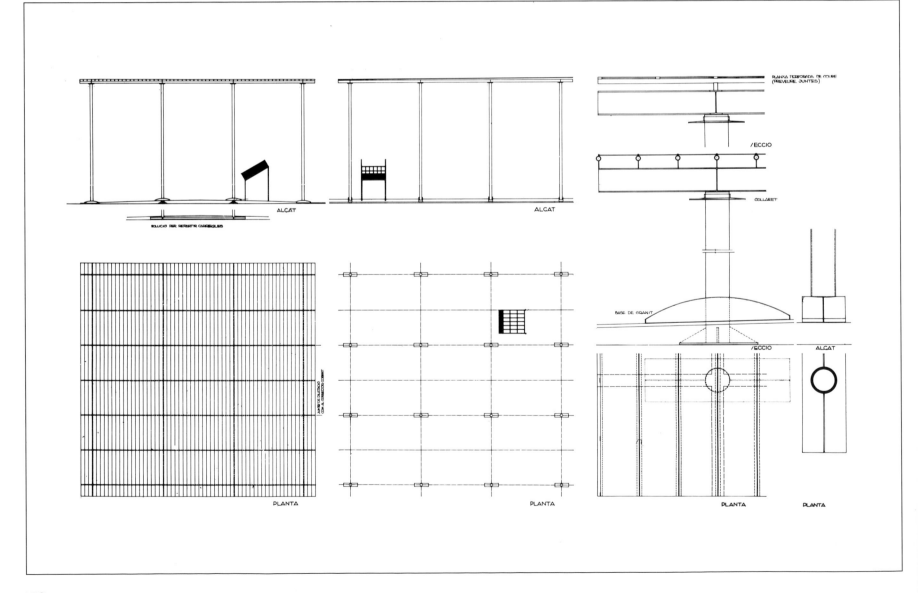

ALCAT

SOLUCIO PER PERMETRE CARREGUES

ALCAT

PLANXA PERFORADA DE COURE
(PREVEURE JUNTES)

/ECCIO

COLLARET

BASE DE GRANIT

/ECCIO

ALCAT

PLANTA

PLANTA

PLANTA

PLANTA

Architect: Santiago Calatrava

Assistants: Pedro Barragán, Bernardo de Solà,
Olga Tarrassó, architects

# Bac de Roda-Felip II bridge

**Barcelona    1984-1987**

The bridge had been conceived as an integral part of the scheme for remodelling an extensive area of Barcelona, situated in a zone bordering on the Cerdà grid. The area, and the bridge, spans the railway line leading to the north of the country. From the urban design point of view, the remodelling project was based on two main interventions: the creation of a large park on either side of the railway line, and the connecting up of two streets – Felip II and Bac de Roda – with the aim of facilitating direct access to the sea. This explains the decision to construct a bridge as the most appropriate solution for creating this link.

On the other hand, the bridge, with a total length of 420 feet and a span of 148 feet, has been treated as an object with an identity of its own, managing to assume the role of a preeminent landmark in its urban context. This is due to the great arches which make it identifiable from a distance, and at the same time give it an exceptional dynamism. The pairs of vertical and inclined arches along with the cables create a space which is mirrored in the central protuberances visible in the plan. By means of these elements, urban spaces have been created – two hanging *piazzas* – which communicate with the park by way of the lateral staircases.

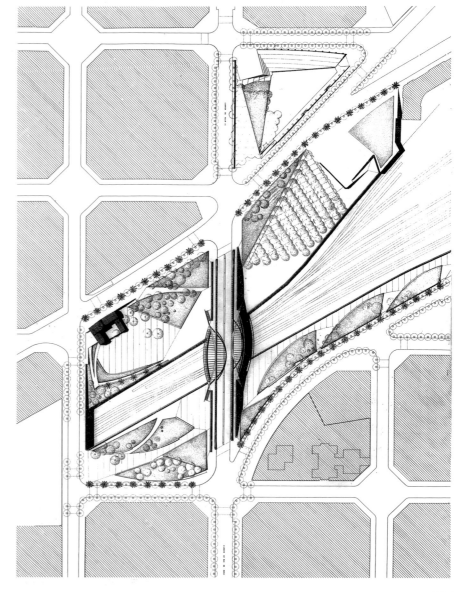

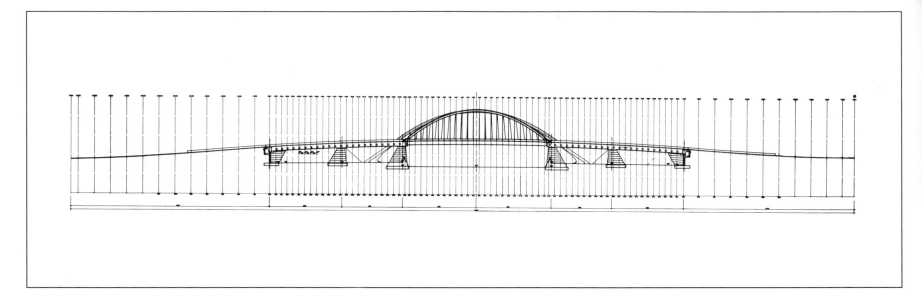

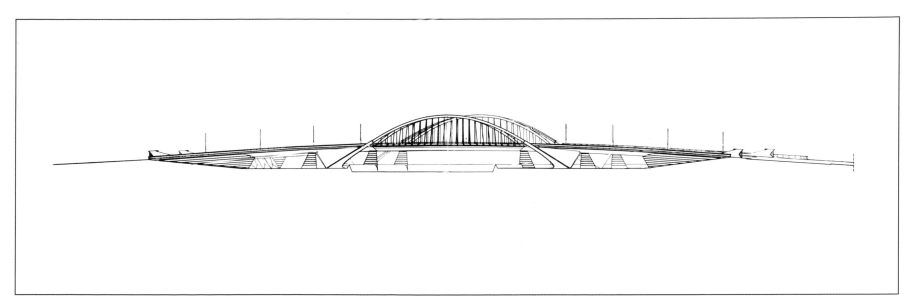

Architects: Pedro Barragán/Bernardo de Solà

Sculpture: Richard Serra

# Plaça de la Palmera

## Barcelona    1982-1984

The project entailed a reconversion of the terrain on the outer fringes of the Cerdà Eixample, between carrers Puigcerdà, Maresme, Andrade and Concili de Trento, in the heart of neighborhood characterized by isolated sixtles buildings. The result makes the Plaça de la Palmera a point of reference for this sector of the city so lacking in urban identity.

The sculptor Richard Serra found himself strongly motivated by the commission, in view of the freedom implicit in taking part in the configuration of the space. He set out – right from his very first exploration of the area – to discover the conditioning factors, the significant features, and the little functional and atmospheric details with which his work would have to coexist: the proud presence of the palm tree, the school nearby, the crumbling industrial structures in the neighborhood, the vertical quality of the apartment blocks and the smell of the saturated red clay.

Two concentric arcs of reinforced concrete, 171 feet long by 10 inches thick, cut fleetingly across the central part of the site, which is divided into two quite separate sectors: the *wood* contained behind the walls, and the *field*, the open space before them. To counteract the silence which might result from this space, the thick wall half opens to reveal the delights of the garden.

The grove of trees, the bandstand in the garden, the palm tree caught within the dynamic dualism of the wall, the cobbled paths spreading radially over the square, for all that they might seem quite foreign, quite unrelated to the incisive sculpture, are laid out in a disciplined fashion, in an effect of sympathetic resonance, following the elementary laws of geometry emanating from the wall.

Only the slender lighting tower rises up emphatically, claiming a leading role. The tree-lined walkways, like a pedestrian avenue, draw together the space and refer it back to the stasis of the surrounding square, which might be used for a future extension of the garden to occupy the rest of the city block.

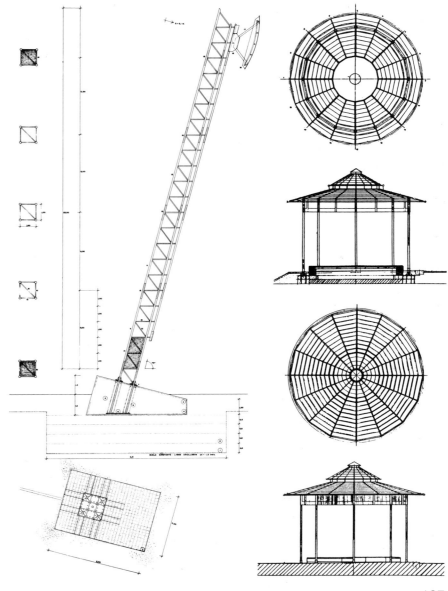

189

# Creueta del Coll Park

Architects: Josep Martorell/Oriol Bohigas/
David Mackay

Assistant: Adolf Martínez, architect

**Barcelona    1981-1987**

A project area of forty one acres is surrounded by dense building, and sits on the upper part of a hill partially taken up by quarry workings. Nowadays, the crater of the abandoned quarry is quite empty, while some other parts of the site have been illegally developed, essentially adjacent to the neighboring streets.

The project organizes the park in two sectors, with clearly differentiated characters. The waste ground of the northern slope, which looks towards Tibidabo, has been treated as land to be reforested, with a basic network of paths which allows the laying out of play areas, picnic areas and a open-air theater. Taking advantage of the structure of the margins of one part of the hillside, the scheme also proposes terraces to accomodate a variety of sports facilities, which connect up with the 4921 square feet piazza specifically designed for the inhabitants of the neighboring La Teixonera district.

On the southern slope, the steps of the main access to the park lead up from the Mare de Deu del Coll Avenue to a 19,685 square feet semicircular piazza, ringed by the walls of the crater. A 328 foot-long pool, which can be used for water-sports competitions, marks the movement from the great esplanade of the piazza to the succession of tiers and terraces which sweep up like an amphitheater to the rim of the crater. A series of gently-climbing paths lead up to the different levels.

The park's sightlines are given additional interest by the presence of three great sculptures. Crowning the end of the entrance ramp is a vertical piece by Ellsworth Kelly. Over the raised lake is a great concrete sculpture by Eduardo Chillida, suspended from four cables fixed directly into the mountainside. On the summit of the hill will be a huge sculpture by Roy Liechtenstein, an immense female face, which will constitute a landmark and point of reference for the whole of this part of Barcelona.

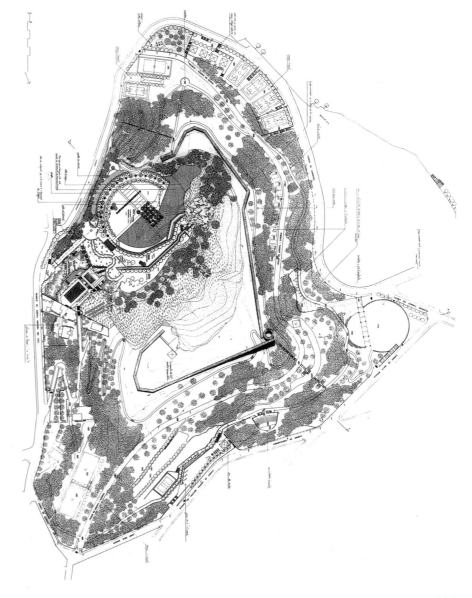

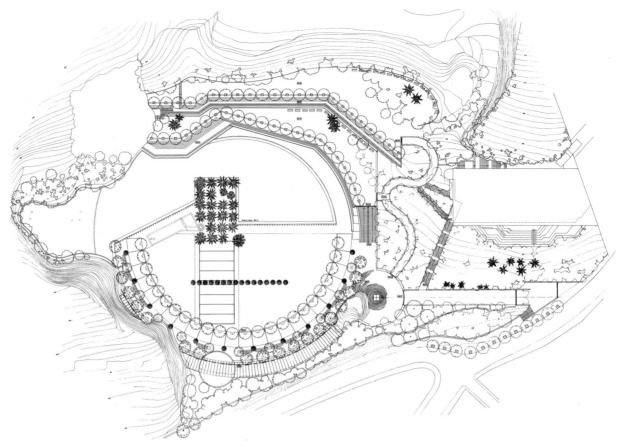

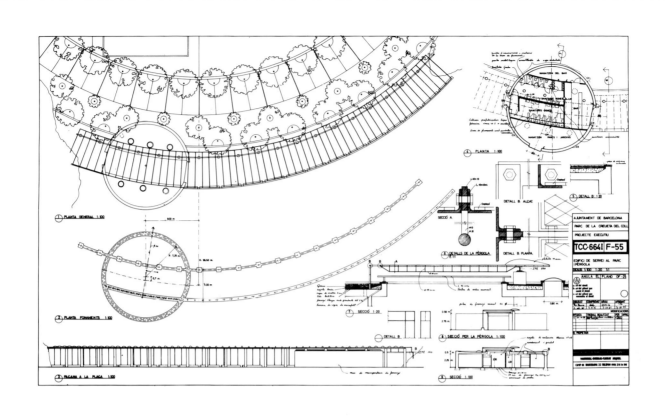

# Hotels/schools/ communications

Hotel Rambla 122

Diagonal Block – Diagonal Building

Hotel Torre Melina

Torre Balldovina nursery school

Conversion of the La Llauna factory as a BUP secondary school

BUP secondary school

Communications tower

Remodelling of the terminal building of Barcelona airport

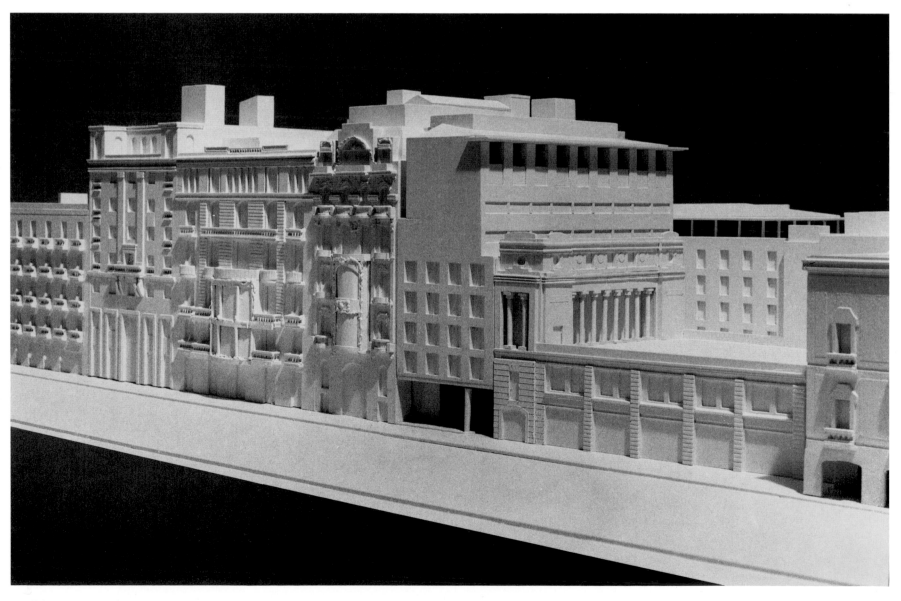

Architects: Esteve Bonell/Josep Maria Gil

Assistants: Marie-Christine Aubry, Desirée Mas, Félix Kuhn

# Hotel Rambla 122

## Barcelona   1988-1992

The present detailed study has been worked out for the city block bounded by the Rambla dels Estudis and carrers Canuda, Bot and Portaferrissa in Barcelona. Its object is the ordering of a new building to be used as a hotel, on a site consisting of a series of plots in the center of the block, with facades on the Rambla and on carrer Bot.

The context in which this revitalizing operation is taking place has an impact on the entire block, as the new building relates to the Ateneu Barcelonès, to the extreme north, as well as to the Moja palace, to the south. The presence of the loggia of the former courtyard of the palace, protected by a conservation order, along with the unusually low height of the commercial premises occupying the former courtyard, which now lies between the palace and the future hotel, also plays a decisive role in the urban context. The plot to be rebuilt will constitute an element of architectonic suturing and local resolution on this unique – even slightly surprising – stretch of the Rambla.

The anticipated scheme, by means of the quality of the design of its facade, disposition of openings, and stonework, has the opportunity of inserting into the Rambla a building which is present-day in conception and execution, intelligently conscious of the site it occupies, and complementary to the rich urban fabric of this area.

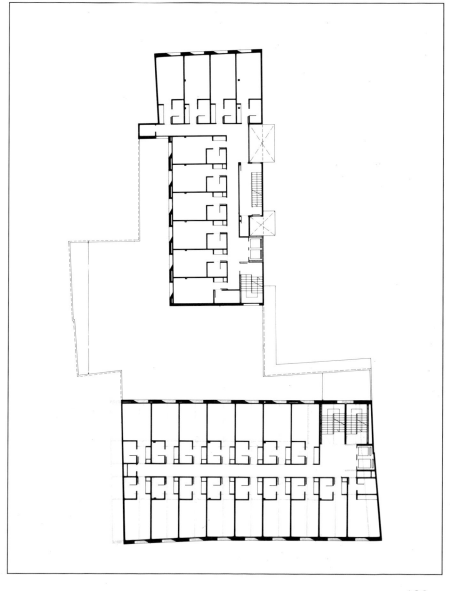

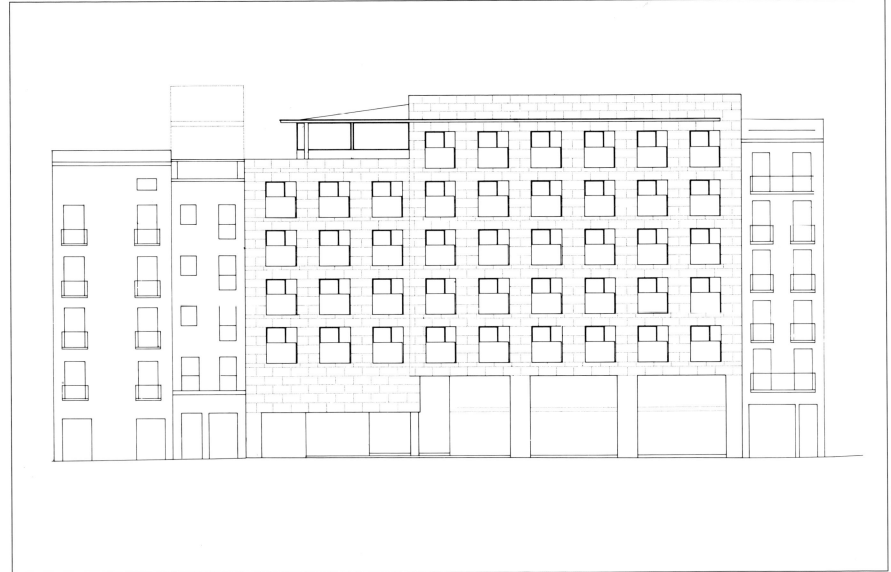

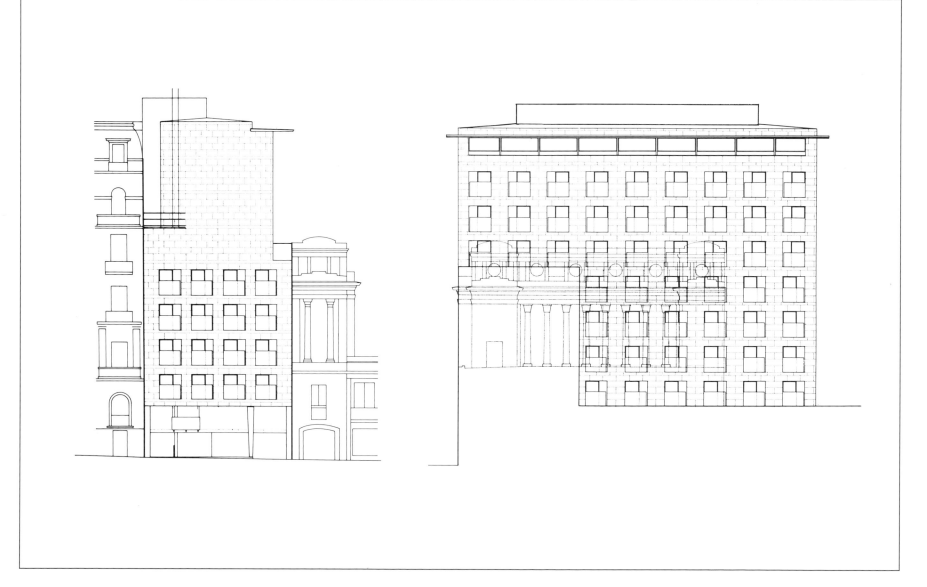

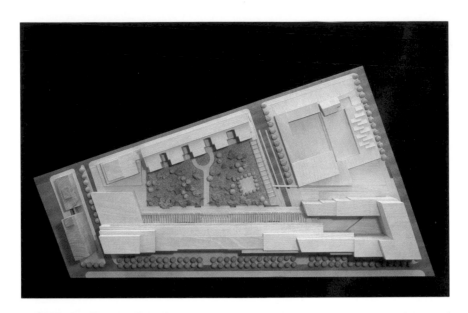

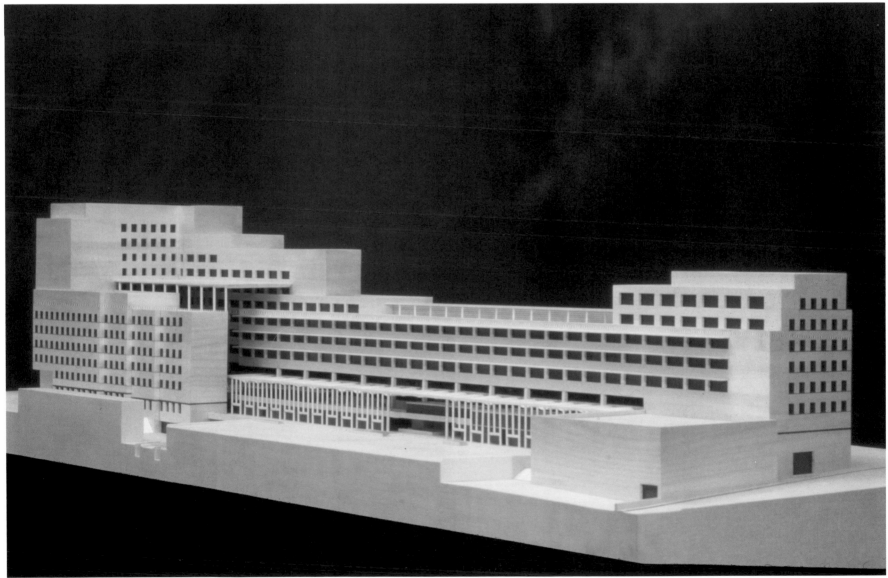

Architects: Manuel de Solà-Morales/Rafael Moneo

Assistants: Lluís Tobella, Andrea Casiraghi,
Mariano Moreno, Sereland

# Diagonal Block – Diagonal Building

## Barcelona    1986-1993

The Diagonal Building takes up the theme of repetition and rationalism characteristic of skyscrapers and very tall buildings, and applies it to a horizontal development more appropriate to the context of the site.

The avenue is formalized with a structure like an urban center, conferred by the presence of a structure on a very grand scale, strong in image and evocation.

The functioning of the Diagonal block has been approached as a center of integrated services: stores, shops, food market, offices, hotel, amusements, restaurants, conference facility, gardens, and car park.

The pavement of the Diagonal has been tripled in surface area and height in order to accomodate all of the uses of one of the city's major centers of activity.

The rigorous aspect of the metropolitan facade along the Diagonal contrasts with the cheerful character of the rear facade which looks onto the peaceful, sunny interior park.

The rationalism which dominates all of the project's architectonic language finds a sensitive aesthetic value in the many details and nuances, elements which create real interest on the small scale, close to the user and visitor.

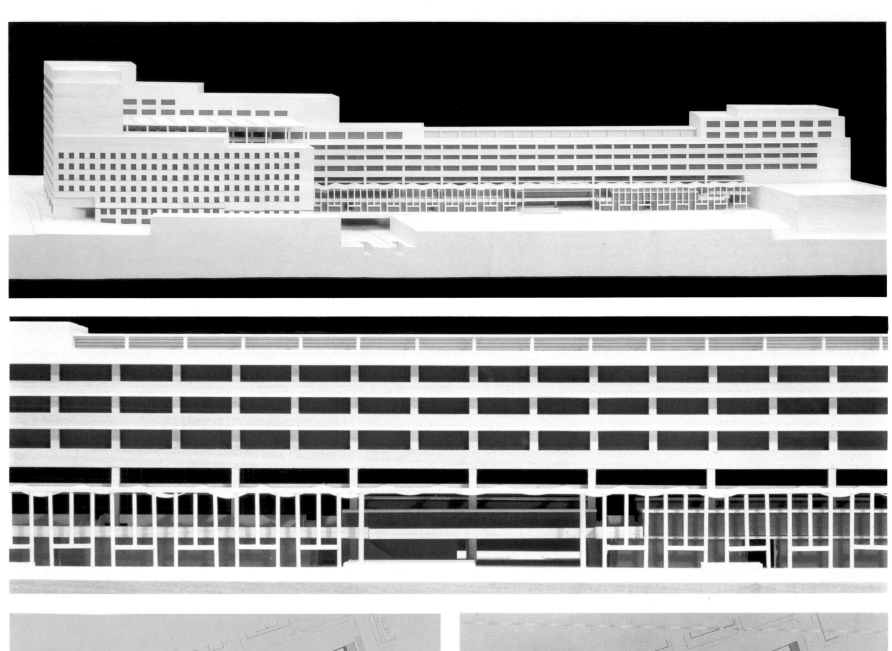

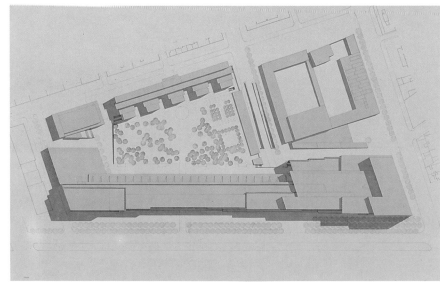
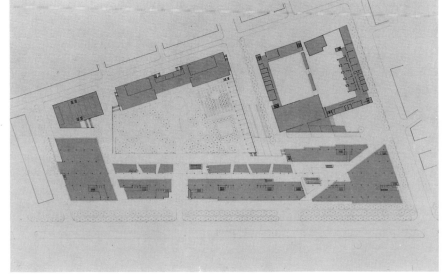

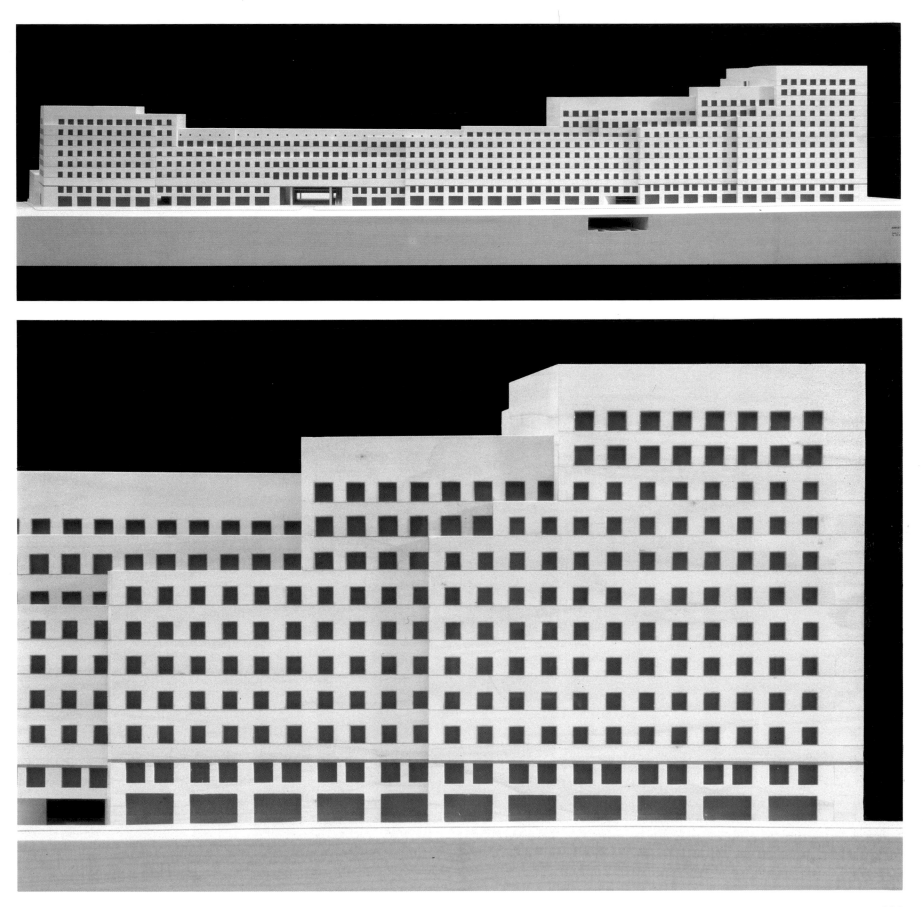

205

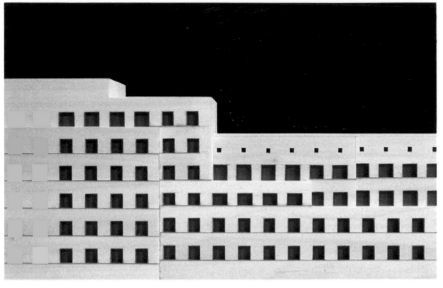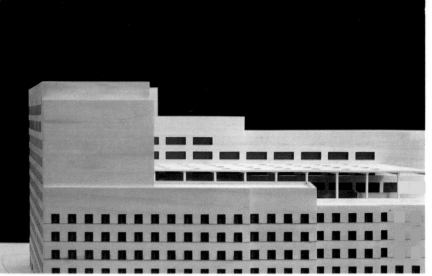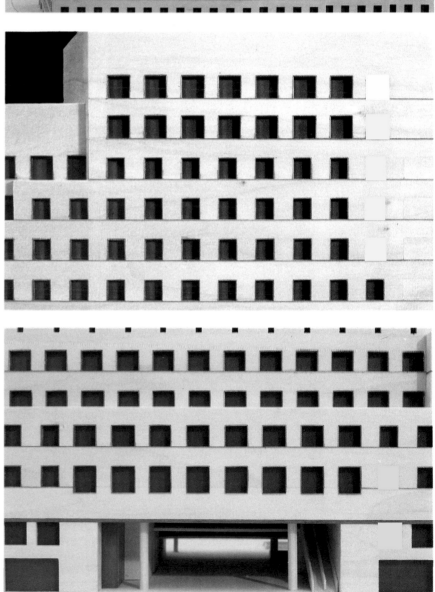

206

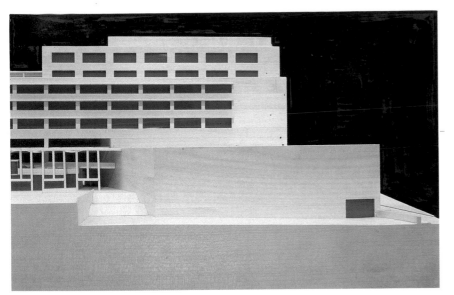

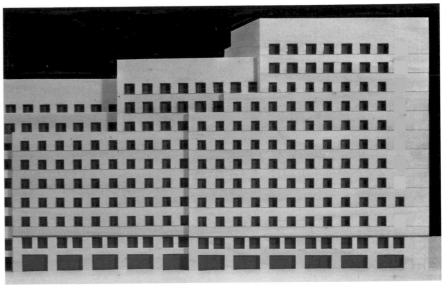

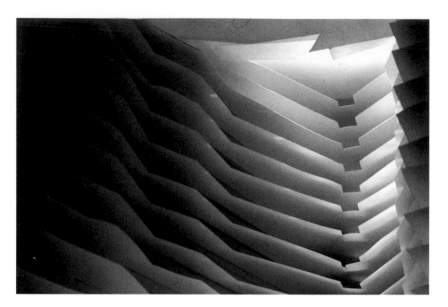

Architect: Carlos Ferrater

Assistant: Josep Maria Cartañà, architect

# Hotel Torre Melina

## Barcelona 1988-1992

On the Diagonal, with a garden by way of an atrium, is the main entrance to the former dog racing track and the Turó tennis club.

The complex is divided into four areas:

In the north-east sector is a health center. This area will be equipped with a surgical clinic with fifteen post-operative rooms, as well as a fitness gymnasium.

The recreation center is located in the south-west sector, consisting of a large function suite with capacity for one thousand people.

On the south-east side is a three hundred seat auditorium, a fifteen hundred person conference hall, a business center, equipped with the most modern facilities, a small shopping center, the tower block housing the EEC suites, an underground car park, and a four hundred room five-star hotel.

At the extreme northern edge of the site two trapezoidal walls help to define the exterior square, supporting the canopies and the large glazed surface which encloses the full-height foyer. The emergency stairs and security and safety services are situated behind the walls.

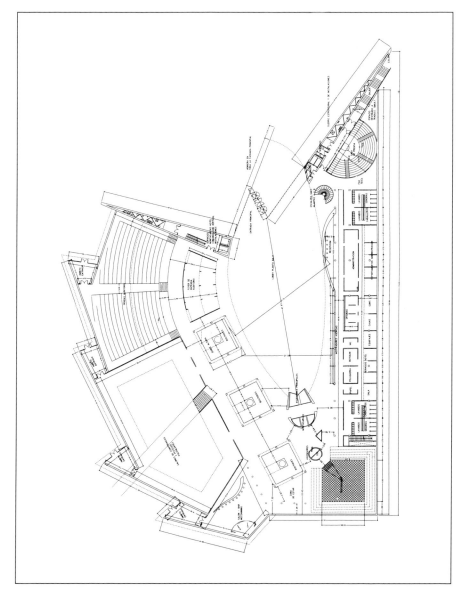

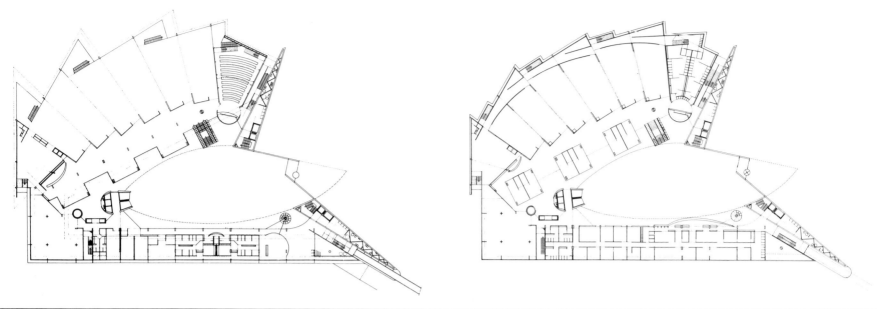

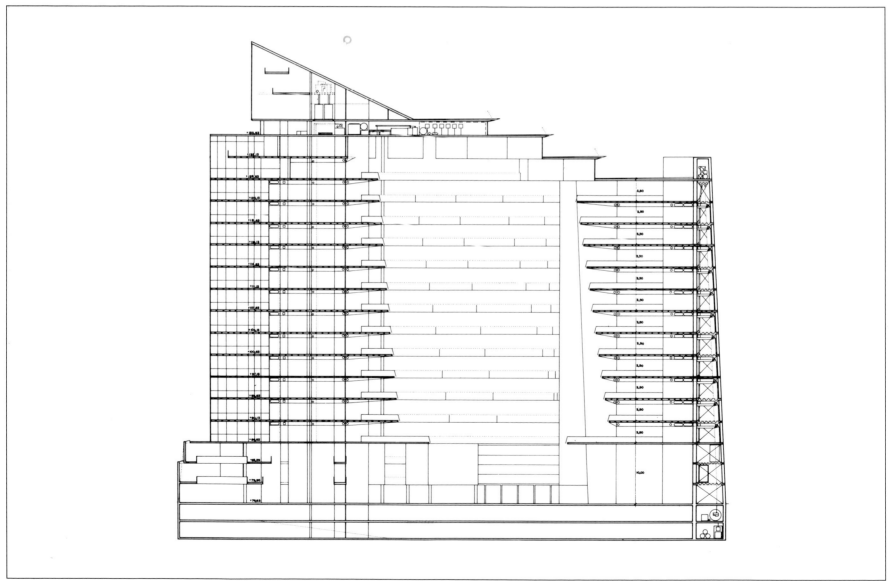

210

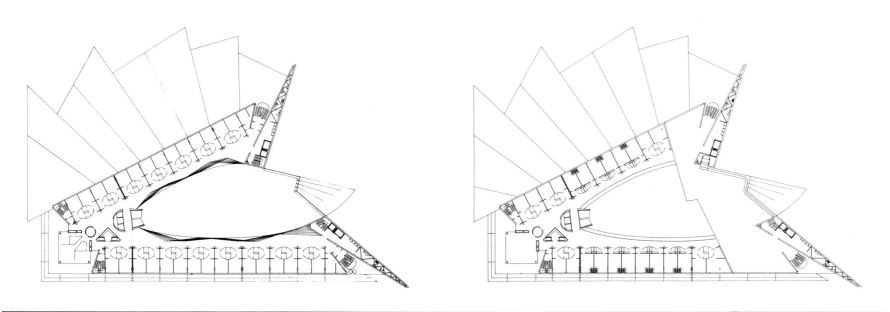

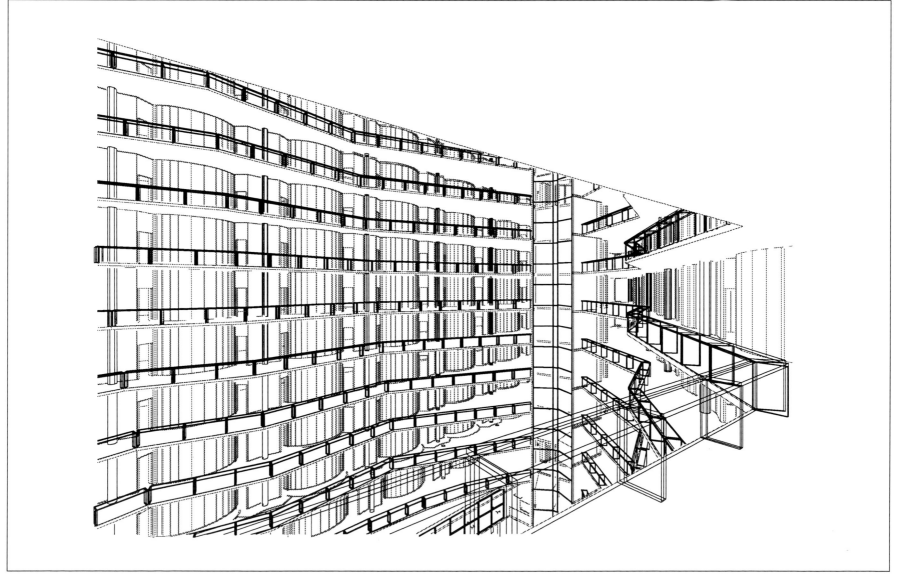

Architects: Jaume Bach/Gabriel Mora

Assistants: Carmina Sanvicens, Adolf Martínez,
Josep Lluís Sisternes, Joan Ardèvol

Structures: Robert Brufau, architect

# Torre Balldovina nursery school

**Santa Coloma de Gramenet,
Barcelona    1985-1987**

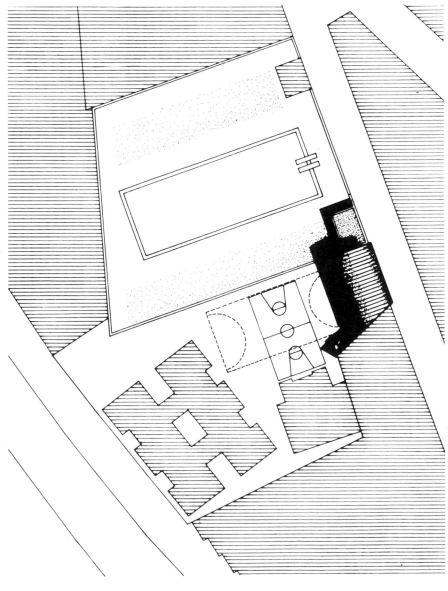

To the rear of a state school constructed in Santa Coloma de Gramenet during the dark years, an area where the city all but fizzles out, a narrow space faces onto the street. It lies between a boundary wall and the side of a squash court of doubtful provenance, which forms part of the neighboring sports area, complete with swimming pool.

In this setting the autonomous goverment of Catalonia, the Generalitat, commissioned a small nursery school, which called for a multi-purpose function hall, four classrooms and a controlled playground.

The program and conditioning factors have been addressed by a building which is stepped up towards the only pleasant view to be found in the vicinity: the sports area and swimming pool, culminating with its own independent roof, which creates a portico on the upper part of the site.

The building progressively extends to cover the gap site, containing an internal staircase as well as a flight of external emergency stairs, which doubles back on itself against the building in order to definitively cover the less than ideal dimensions of the site.

The two facades produced by the stepping of the building are similar to one another, with the north facade being differentiated by the addition of capricious catwalks serving the solidly-built mass of the emergency stairs.

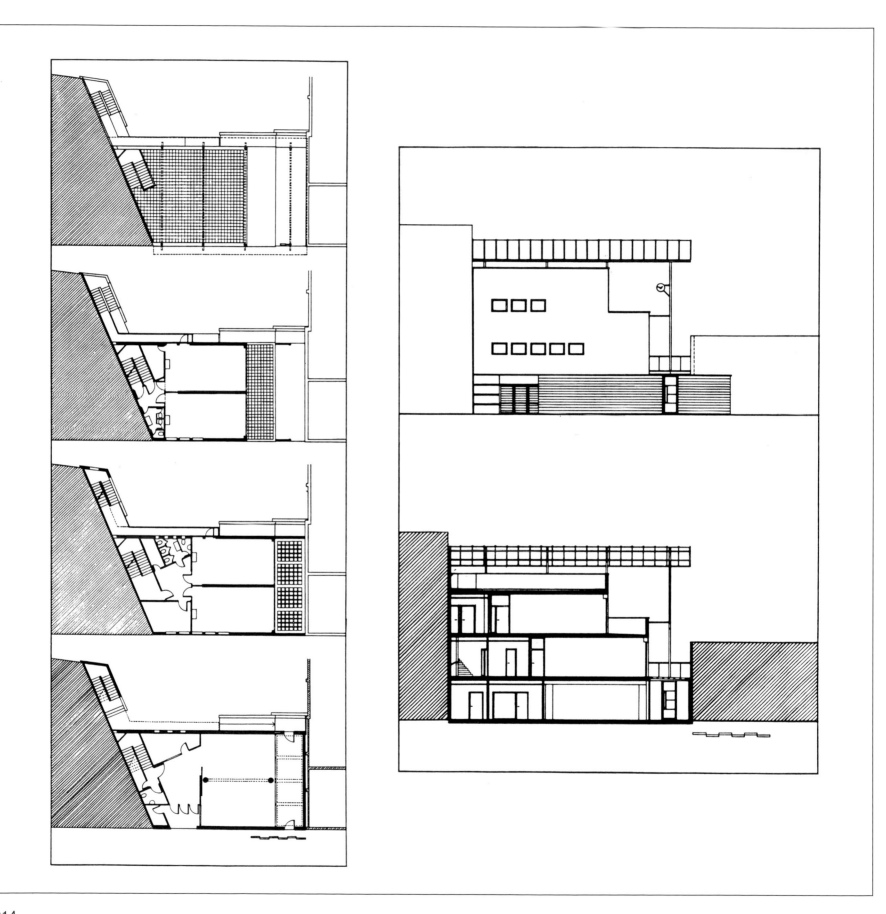

Architects: Enric Miralles/Carme Pinós

Structures: Robert Brufau, Agustí Obiols, architects

# Conversion of the La Llauna factory as a BUP secondary school

## Badalona, Barcelona    1984-1986

The various different proposals for the remodelling of the old
G. Andreis Metalgraf Española factory (1906-1919), the work of the
*Modernista* architect Joan Amigó Barriga, were organized into a single
project. This formed the basis for a number of decisions which, in
influencing the accesses, contributed directly to the construction of the
space. There was no time to design the project... That makes it special.
The photographs are the drawings which allowed us to rediscover
these decisions directly, without intermediaries...

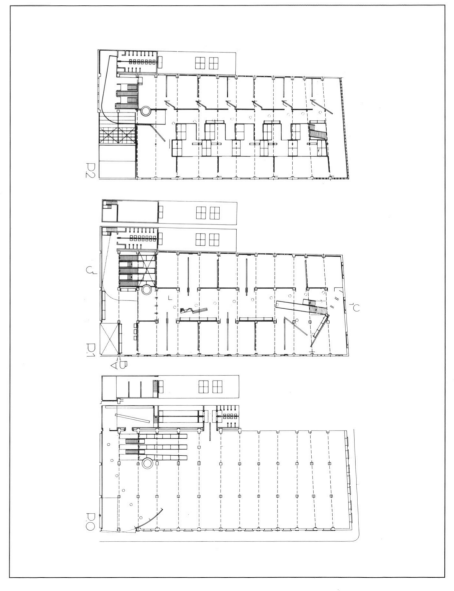

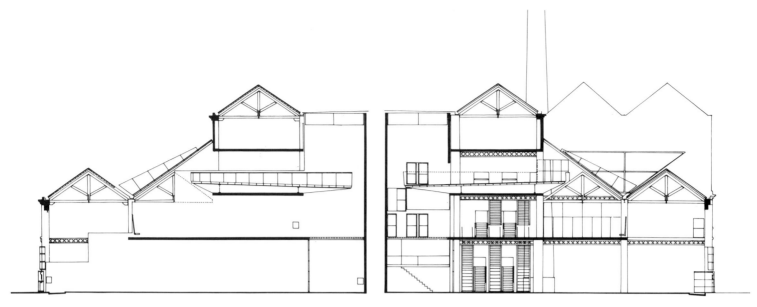

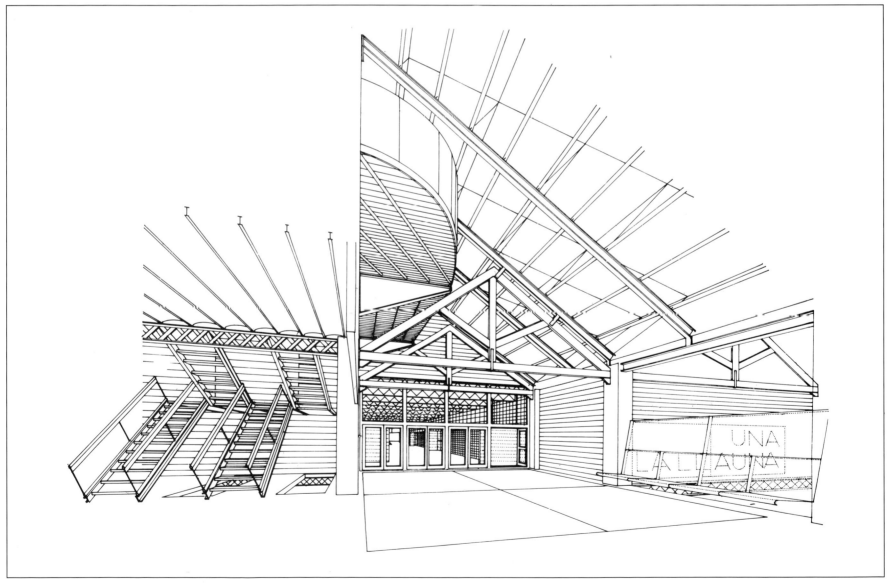

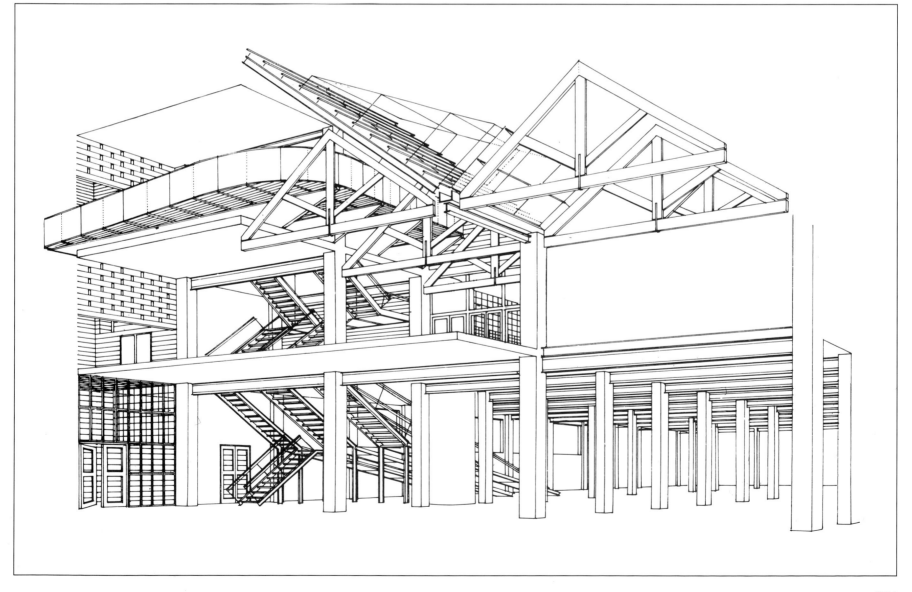

224

Architects: Josep Martorell/Oriol Bohigas/David Mackay

# BUP secondary school

## Sant Adrià de Besòs, Barcelona    1983-1988

The building belongs to a group of three schools planned to stand alongside each other, forming an institutional facade for the town of Sant Adrià de Besòs, and running along the bank of the seasonal river Besòs.

The Escola Catalunya, the first of the three, completed in 1983, left a vacante space next to the BUP secondary school, to be occupied in the future by the third building. All three schools are interrelated by way of an internal pedestrian "street" flanked on either side by classrooms.

The present building, a secondary school for six to seven hundred pupils, is a unitary complex, compact despite its linearity, in the form of a prefabricated structural shell, and as such is both regular and modular. The interior, however, running longitudinally parallel to the river Besòs, is articulated with a succession of spaces of different forms and dimensions, in accordance with the uses called for in the program for the school.

The spatial unity of the building is modified in form and expression when these spaces extend beyond the established outline, or when a volumetric indentation into the interior is deliberately brought about.

On the exterior, the dominant volumetric simplicity is a response to the conditioning factors, at once aggressive and primary, of the suburban setting. In the interior, the complexity and resonance of the spatial sequences respond to the building's functional requirements, and the use of typically urban elements, such as the street and square, to articulate the space. The internal street, triple height and of considerable dimensions, communicates with the exterior at ground floor level at either end, as well as laterally by way of the playground. This multiplicity of accesses facilitates the various different distribution systems a school requires. The classrooms and laboratories, necessarily set apart, resemble houses lined along a street. The dimensions and spatial structure of the interior street qualitatively enrich the corridor-school scheme. At its southern extreme, the street opens out into a square-like area for communal group activities, ascending a flight of steps to arrive at the roof spaces of the east portico.

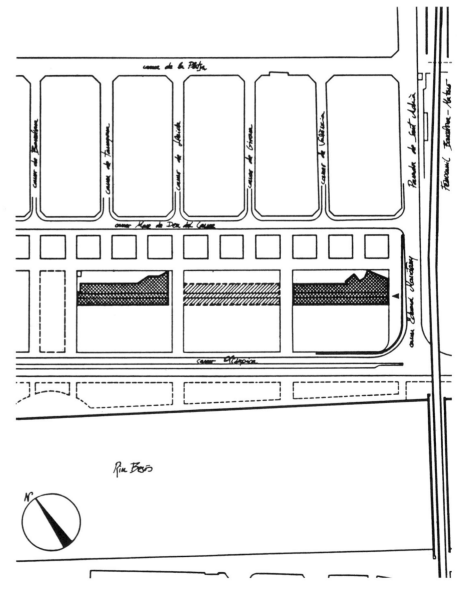

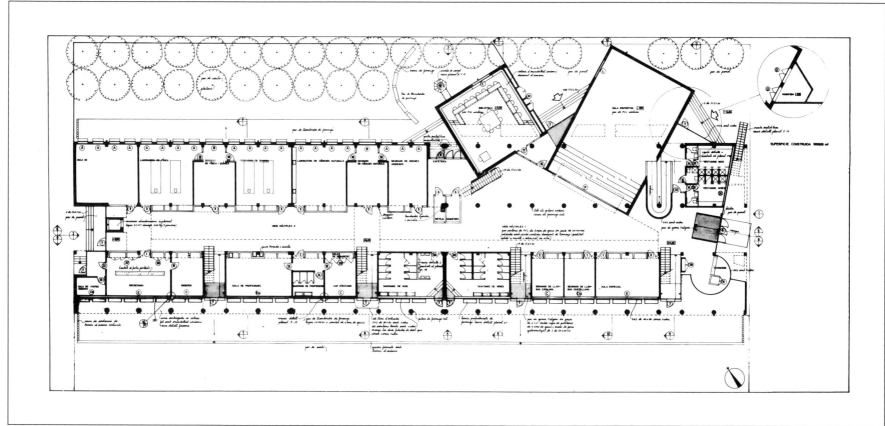

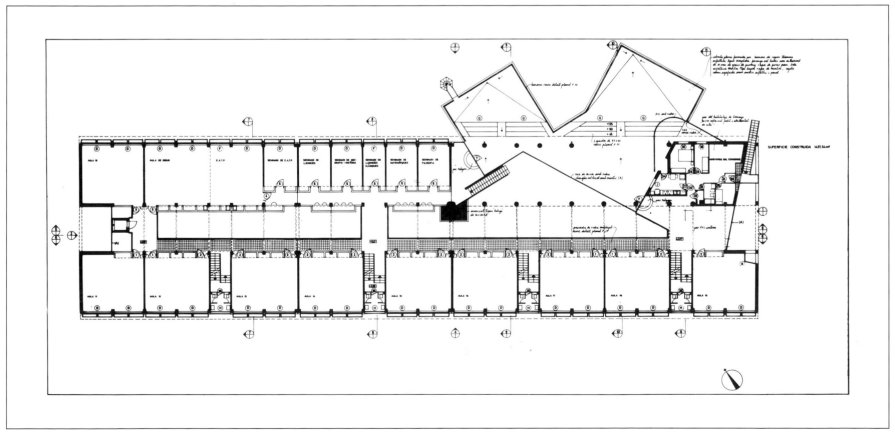

Architect: Norman Foster

Assistants: Ove Arup & Partners, engineering;
Cast, site supervision

# Communications tower

## Collserola, Barcelona    1989-1992

The project for the Barcelona communications tower won a limited competition in July 1988. The structure, which will be completed in time for the 1992 Olympic Games, occupies an outstanding position on the summit of the mountain overlooking the city.

The design of the tower is faithful to Foster's philosophy, based on achieving the maximum of effect with the minimum of structural means. The starting point is a slender shaft – reminiscent of a ship's mast or a flagpole – of precast concrete, standing on a base. This central nucleus is held in place by three vertical supports, one every 120°, and this structural complex is anchored by means of tensile cables fixed into the hillside. The modular framework and the platforms of the tower are suspended from this structural skeleton, composed of the shaft and the system which takes the strain, and have been designed with a view to flexibility, and to allow for possible future alterations. The form of the plan – an equilateral triangle with curving sides – has been designed to offer minimum resistance to the wind and maximum resistance to lateral tension, torsion and vibration. Considerable attention has been paid to questions of safety and maintenance. The lifts, stairs and cables are grouped on the exterior of the central shaft for ease of access, and the high-resistance tensile struts have been designed in such a way that up to one third of the cables of which they are composed can be taken out of service for inspection or replacement, without weakening the stability of the structure. Each of the three anchor-points in the rock has a triple anti-corrosion system. The anchor-bolt is encased in polyester resin, surrounded by a polypropylene skin, and, finally, embedded in concrete. As protection against vandalism, the top and bottom sections of the three main tensors are protected by elastic sleeves, and the whole complex will be equipped with closed circuit TV and a movement detector.

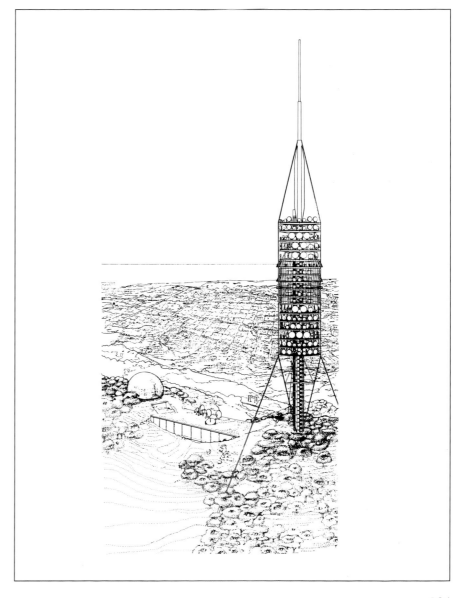

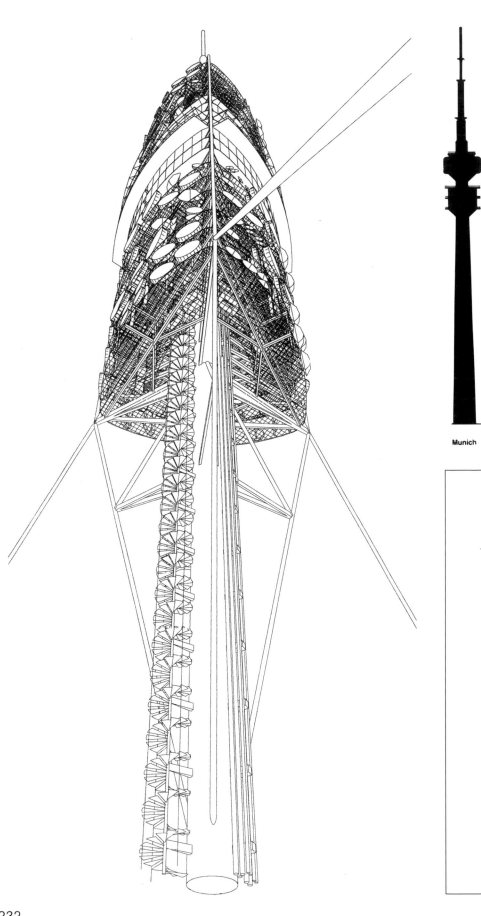

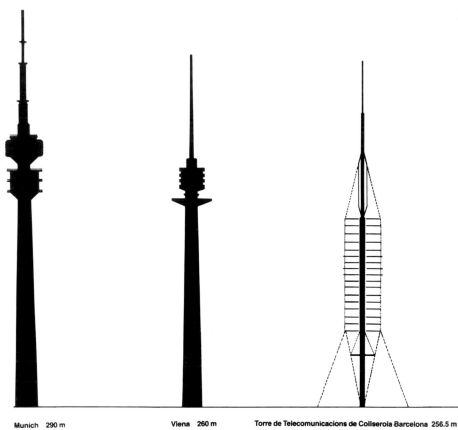

Munich 290 m      Viena 260 m      Torre de Telecomunicacions de Collserola Barcelona 256.5 m

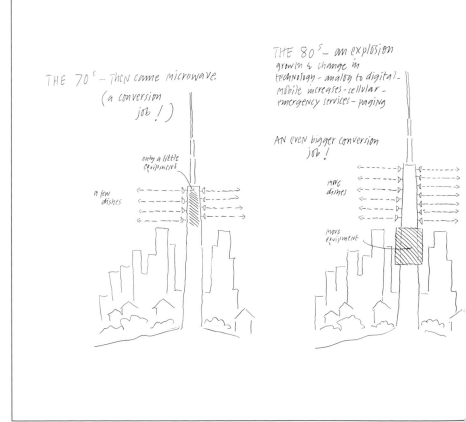

THE 70's – then came microwave. (a conversion job !)

a few dishes

only a little equipment

THE 80's – an explosion growth & change in technology – analog to digital – mobile increases – cellular – emergency services – paging

AN even bigger conversion job !

more dishes

more equipment

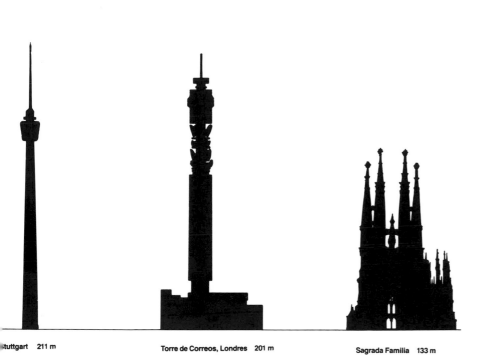

Stuttgart   211 m

Torre de Correos, Londres   201 m

Sagrada Familia   133 m

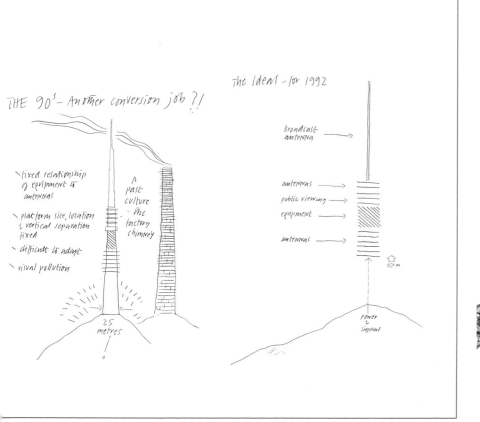

THE 90's - Another conversion job ?!

fixed relationship of equipment & antennas

platform size, location & vertical separation fixed

difficult to adapt

visual pollution

25 metres

A past culture - the factory chimney

The Ideal - for 1992

Broadcast antenna

antennas

public viewing

equipment

antennas

57 m

power & signal

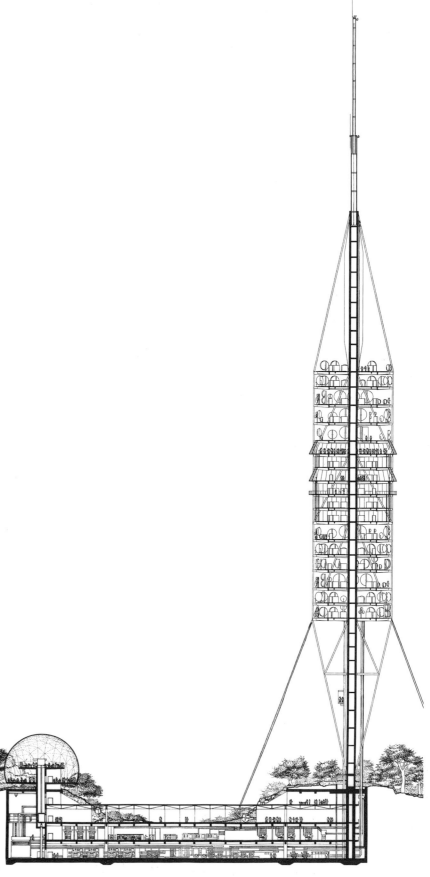

233

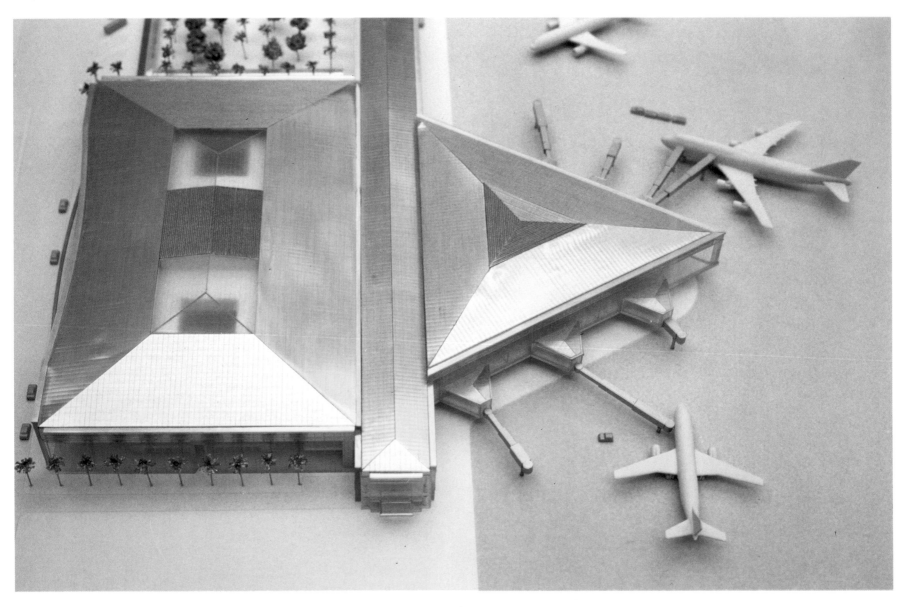

Architect: Ricardo Bofill – Taller de Arquitectura, Intecsa

Ministerio de Transportes, Turismo y Comunicaciones,
Organismo Autónomo Aeropuertos Nacionales

# Remodelling of the terminal building of Barcelona airport

## El Prat de Llobregat, Barcelona    1988-1992

The design of an airport is especially important, as it is the first image to greet the traveller arriving to the city. An airport has the role of gateway to the city, but is also a mirror in which the city should be reflected. This image is then translated into an idea of, and opinion about, the city and the country being visited.

There are two separate and clearly defined zones in an airport: the land side, with all the services and facilities for the passengers, and the air side containing the runways and the technical facilities for the servicing and maintenance of the aircraft.

The basic objectives to be achieved by the remodelling of the airport are to permit a greater volume of traffic, both of passengers and aircraft, and ensure a higher level of comfort. It is anticipated that the volume will rise from the present figure of some six million passengers each year to around twelve million, with an increase in capacity for the number of planes on the ground from thirty-four to sixty two, twenty-four of which will be in contact with the terminal by means of the individual gates.

The air-side facade will be completely new, covering over the existing building with a street and four boarding modules projecting out onto the apron. The triangular modules are designed to accomodate pre-flight lounges with capacity for fifteen hundred passengers to wait in comfort. While waiting for their flight to be called, passengers will have access to amenities such as bars, shops, toilets and telephones.

The land-side facade will present, in the foreground, the new technical block, the existing terminal with a renovated facade, and the new international terminal, all of which will be linked by an elevated walkway running behind them. There will be a passageway under a pergola between the national and international terminals, and gardens and car parking will be laid out along the entire length of the facade.

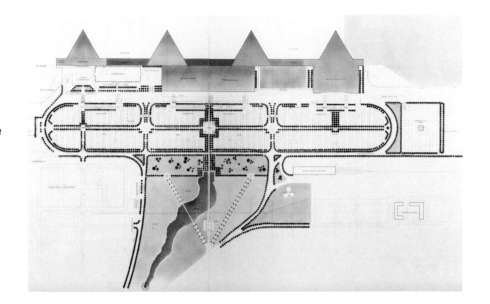

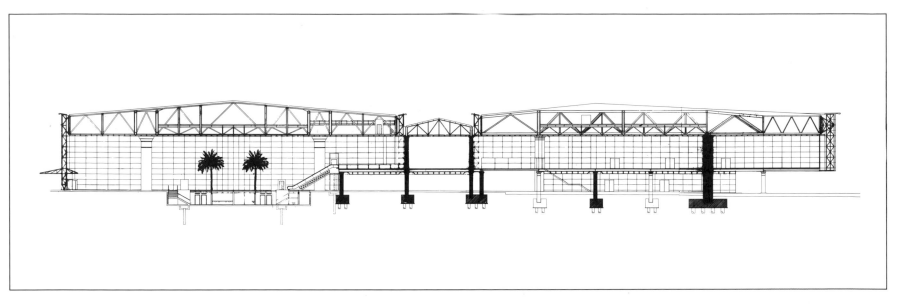

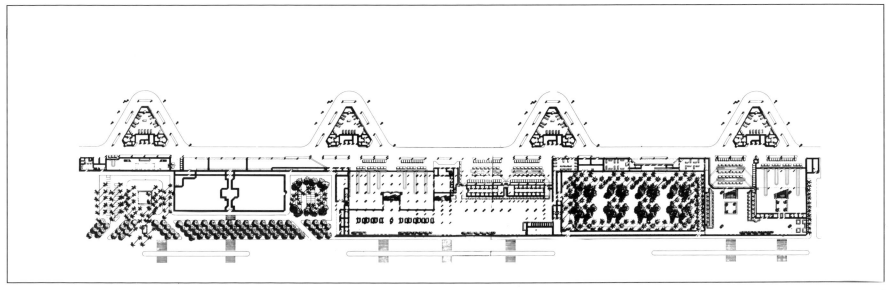

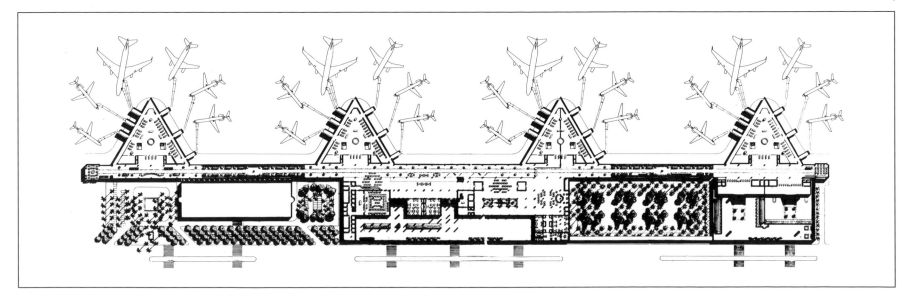

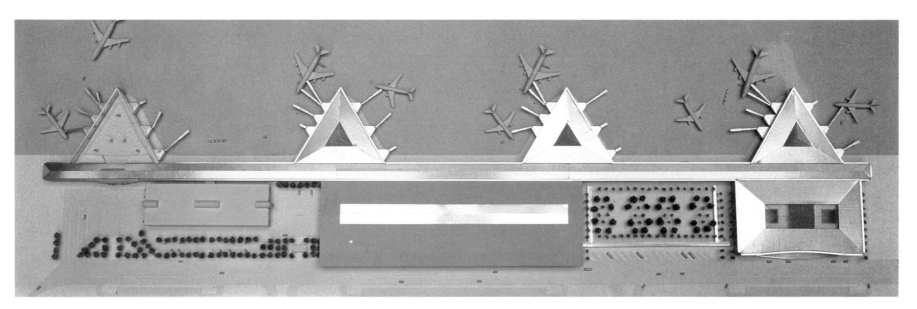

# Photography Credits

# Acknowledgments

The reproduction of the graphic material which accompanies each one
of the projects presented here has been possible thanks, in large part,
to the cooperation of the architects themselves, and of the following
individuals:

Pilar Blanco
Maria Bohigas
Ana G. Cabezali
Sílvia Calavera
Lluís Carreras
Valerià Datzira
Lisa Green
Francesc Gual
Desirée Mas Rigal
Fiona Millar
Polly Napper
Ton Salvador
Francesc Santacana
Frédéric Sanz
Paulina Soucheiron
Mònica Vila